ISLAM'S CLIMATE FOR BUSINESS SUCCESS

W. DEEN MOHAMMED

Library of Congress Cataloging in Publication Data
Mohammed, W. Deen, 1933
Library of Congress Catalog Card Number: 95-071105

ISLAM'S CLIMATE FOR BUSINESS SUCCESS

Cover Design, Layout, Typography and Photos:
Atique Mahmood

Manuscript Preparation:
Ayesha K. Mustafaa & NGina Muhammad

Indexing: Mansur Abdullah

Typesetting: NGina Muhammad

Dialogue: Abdul Mujib T. Mannan

Publisher: The Sense Maker
910 W. Van Buren, First Floor
Chicago, Illinois 60607

Copyright 1995: W. Deen Mohammed
All Rights Reserved. No part of this publication may be reproduced or transmitted in any form or by any means, electronic or mechanical, including photocopy, recording, or any other information storage and retrieval systems without the expressed written permission from the author.
Printed in Chicago, at COLORON by Atique Mahmood

TABLE OF CONTENT

	Foreword	
1	A Concept of The Destiny	9
2	The Common Person Dealing With Perception	27
3	The Promotion of Race and Business, How The Conflict Is Resolved	40
4	Priorities For An Advancing People	58
5	Prepare To Make It In The Land of Plenty	69
6	Managing The Spiritual And The Material	88
7	Protecting The Business Future Upon Sound Motivations	102
	Dialogue	126
	Index	134

FOREWORD

This book, Islam's Climate For Business Success, by Imam W. Deen Mohammed encompasses the principles of the religion of Al-Islam within the context of the climate those principles cultivate. He incorporates the concepts of fairness in trade and strong families as classics held high in Islamic beliefs. They are treated as revolutionary catalysts in the lives of those so obviously impacted by community blight and non-productivity.

The lifestyle of the Muslim, in itself, is a revolution for the oppressed, setting them free of degrading influences, a revolution that implores responsibility for one's self at all times. It is a new lifestyle that resolves the social conflicts of high crime and family breakdown. On the pages of world history - if accurately written - Muslims are noted to have furthered the spread of their religion via the avenues of trade, not by the sword - as many historians we shall say misconceived.

Islam inspires the human intellect and frees its soul, making for fertile grounds for the inherent potential of man (and woman) to burst forth. This book by Imam Mohammed explains some influences affecting this process of enlightenment that sparks such growth inspired by the Qur'an and the Life Examples of Prophet Muhammed, the prayers and peace be on the Prophet.

But not only does W. Deen Mohammed write about these lofty traditions of crystal clear Islam, he also has exemplified them in his own business and social interactions. Wherever he could, he has improved the living standards for the commoner. He has reached out to aid children and the widowed. Before "job sharing" was an American corporate concept, he exercised this form of consideration to make the work place family friendly. He has been one to follow in Prophet Muhammed's tradition to "pay the worker while the sweat is still on his brow." He has been adamant about building an economically sound community from the bottom up - with the worker benefitting from his own investments, rather than from the top downward, where those on the ground level hardly ever experience the sweet tasting fruits of their own labor.

Now celebrating twenty years of continuous leadership for a community of Muslim Americans who emerged from the old Nation of Islam built by his father, the Hon. Elijah Muhammad, Imam Mohammed has withstood the test of time. He is the same "Wallace" today that he was as a young man under his father's influence but not controlled by anyone. He is one who chose to go the way of "truth" even at the expense of losing the comfort he once knew in his father's home.

Those who have been waiting to see some other character take over this man we have come to know as Imam W. Deen Mohammed have gone about in their great disappointment, for he is the same today as he was during the days when his father exiled him from the Nation of Islam: A man that puts faith over matter and principles over material gain and God above it all. He resisted the tendencies of his constituents to continue in the pattern of the old Nation of Islam by elevating its leaders to "godly" stations. It was W. Deen Mohammed who pointed them to the pure concept of God being the Creator of all and not affected by or contained within His Own creation. Imam Mohammed said to the former members of the Nation of Islam: "False worship is the worst oppression." (The Qur'an)

Imam Mohammed has lived a lifestyle of austerity. He ministers that the acquisition of wealth is for the good of the whole and not to be put to exaggerated self adorations. The text of this book encompasses those lectures given by Imam Mohammed all across the United States in his contribution to improve the "climate for success" of America's less fortunate and to improve the "climate to retain dignity" for America's wavering achievers - be it through moral dilemma or economically unsound decision making.

He began this particular series of lectures focusing on the business community and economic interests for Muslims on March 19, 1989, in Dallas, Texas, preparing his audience to "make it in the land of plenty."

In Bridgeport, Connecticut, on June 10, 1989, he gave a public address with emphasis on how the Qur'an addresses business interests.

On December 3, 1989, in Detroit, Michigan, he stressed the need to manage spiritual and material needs.

Continuing his campaign to resolve the conflict over promoting business achievement and race pride, he addressed the public in Atlanta, Georgia, on September 2, 1990.

He returned to Atlanta on December 30, 1990, and spoke on the role of business in Muslim life.

In Nashville, Tennessee, on May 26, 1991, the Imam gave a public address on the value of strong families to the prospects of business success.

On February 23, 1992, the Imam gave a public address in Birmingham, Alabama, on the real meaning of success.

He then returned to Dallas, Texas, on May 23, 1992, and spoke on common sense perceptions.

In Chicago, Illinois, on November 14, 1992, the Imam addressed "The Muslim Life, Our Priorities for Sharing Life and Responsibility in the City."

The culmination of this book is with the text of his public address, in part, at the National Muslim Business Conference held in Newark, New Jersey, on May 28, 1995. His topic in Newark was "Business Owners Club and Muslim Business Community Supporting Schools and Business Progress."

Also used are excerpts from his public address given on August 13, 1995, in Detroit, Michigan, where the theme of his lecture was "Islam in America, The African American Future."

This foreword does not represent the full scope of ministering, educating, meeting, dialoguing, planning and coalition building that Imam W. Deen Mohammed has done within any one of these years and others in between. His speaking calendar puts to stress the young-at-heart as well as the dedicated to keep abreast of his many, many endeavors to serve his community, his co-citizens, his brothers and sisters in the faith, this humanity that God raised him in. These lectures deserve serious study and for that purpose are presented in this one text.

(Ayesha K. Mustafaa, Editor of the Muslim Journal; BA

Degree with a Double Major in Psychology and Political Science from Bucknell University, Lewisburg, Penn.; Master's Degree in Newsprint Journalism from Columbia College, Chicago, Illinois; October, 1995.)

Ar-Rahman: *The Merciful Benefactor*

With Allah's Name, The Merciful Benefactor, The Merciful Redeemer

1. (God) Most Gracious!
2. It is He Who has taught the Qur'an.
3. He has created man:
4. He has taught him speech (and Intelligence).
5. The sun and the moon
follow courses (exactly) computed;
6. And the herbs and the trees -
both (alike) bow in adoration.
7. And the Firmament has He raised high,
and He has set up The Balance (of Justice),
8. In order that ye may
not transgress (due) balance.
9. So establish weight with justice
and fall not short in the balance.
10. It is He Who has spread out
the earth for (His) creatures:
11. Therein is fruit and date-palms,
producing spathes (enclosing dates);
12. Also corn, with (its) leaves and stalk for fodder,
and sweet-smelling plants.
13. Then which of the favors of your Lord will ye
deny?....

(QUR'AN, CHAPTER 55)

ISLAM'S CLIMATE FOR BUSINESS SUCCESS

A Concept of The Destiny

As-Salaam-Alaikum. That is peace be unto you. We always like to begin by giving recognition to Allah (God) Who is responsible for everything that is good and is responsible for all the benefits that we receive. Giving recognition to Him, we say "With Allah's Name, the Merciful Benefactor, the Merciful Redeemer." We give thanks to Him for the blessing of the last and universal Prophet Muhammed, upon him be peace and prayers and what follows of the best salutation.

The Role of Al-lslam in Promoting Business Development

I'm going to begin with certain quotes from the Qur'an. It is the Islamic scholars' tradition that we first give these verses in Arabic, whether the speaker himself knows what he is saying or not. The speaker is supposed to give what is said in the Qur'an first in its original text as it is in the Arabic. I thank Allah that I do know the Arabic quotes and their meanings, and I will be referring to several surahs (chapters) in the Qur'an. "For those who do good in this world, there is good." In other words, the blessings of good is guaranteed. If you do good, you are going to receive good. We know that is also common language and common knowledge of the good and morally upright people, for we all think that to do good is to get good. I have heard that so many times on the streets, in homes, and from my teachers.

This quote is from Chapter 16 of the Qur'an: "And certainly the home of the destiny is best for those who are regardful." We are to recognize the Lord Creator (Allah) as being uppermost in the attention to regardfulness. It continues: "Then will you not be informed?" Another quote from the Holy Qur'an reads: "That special home of the destiny, We have made it for those who do not want dominance over the earth and who do not want to make corruption." Allah also says in the Qur'an, "And seek by the means that Allah has availed you the home of the destiny. However do not forget your share of this world." Prophet Muhammed has said, peace and blessings be upon him: "Live in the world as though you are going to die tomorrow. And live as though you will never die."

I want to come back to some key words in these quotes from Qur'an. "Ahsanu" simply translated means "they do good." A teacher tells his student when that student has excelled, "Ahsanta." It means that you have done excellent. There are many other Arabic terms for the expression "good." "Ahsanu" means they have done good in the spirit of goodness and human excellence. For those who do that in this world there is "hasana." Allah is assuring us, if we perform excellently, strive for excellence, we are going to have excellence to our credit in the world. If we strive for excellence in business, according to what Allah says here, we are to have excellent results in business in this world. We will have excellence to our credit as business persons. Our religion addresses the concerns of business and all material benefits. It is concern for a balanced life. Mind you, we want to keep the emphasis on "the destiny."

For us "the destiny" is to be understood mainly in two ways. There is the common way that the great religions understand destiny, in that we have to meet Allah one day. We have to account for our lives and for how we lived or how we conducted ourselves. If we have done good, we expect to be rewarded accordingly. The reward for that is a place in Paradise or in heaven, which is a blissful life, an eternally happy life. Yet it is a life on a different plane, in a different dimension. However, "the destiny" is also to be understood in this life.

The Muslim's concept of hell and heaven is different from the concept of hell and heaven given in most religions, as I understand them. Our (Muslim) concept is different in that we believe we experience both conditions of heaven and hell in this life, and Allah rewards us with both in this life. What we do of evil will earn for us a hell on this earth at the address where we live now. At that address the hell will come. Muslims also believe that if we manage our life as Allah intended, also at that address the heaven will start. We believe that both heaven and hell are conditions that start in this very life, although Allah says you will not get the fullness of it until the resurrection. You will not see hell in full, you will not see heaven in its fullness until the resurrection. But here in this lifetime you get a little of both. Some may say, "Well I have gotten enough of hell already, and I don't expect any more." And I want to agree with you, you probably will not get any more. Some people have been punished so much by sins in this life, that I don't think they will get anymore hell. But they must turn around their lives, please.

Allah, through His Book, Qur'an, informs us that if we do good and strive and work for excellence in this world, we are going to receive excellence and get the result of excellence to our credit, recognition and enjoyment. This is also addressing business people. If business people work for excellence in their business, then their business will be seen for excellence. People will associate the person and the business with excellence. It will be said: "You have an excellent product; you give excellent service." But that recognition doesn't come unless you strive for it in the spirit of excellence and goodness.

Let's look again at what Allah says, that the home of the destiny is "khair." And the term "khair" is translated as "best, better and good." "Khair" is a strong word for what is good and is distinguished from other terms that mean good. "Khair" means "useful" also, not only what is "useful" to one person, but what is useful to everybody. It is not only "useful" in one town, but in all towns. Not just in this country, but in all countries. It means that which is claimed by everybody as being good and useful, with universal value. It is seen as good and useful universally - by all nations, by all people. There are times when we will have something and claim it to be so good. And perhaps it is that good, but it does not mean that it is good for everybody. We may go just next door and offer it there and the house next door will not want it. So Allah in calling us to "khair" calls us to what is best and of universal value.

We have another idea about the destiny. We believe Allah points us to the destiny to tell us that to work for the "future good" is best. To look to the future for results and for establishment and to plan the long range plan is better than the disposition to have immediate, quick, "benefit-me-now" results. As business

11

persons, we will know that to be true. The quick plan just for today or just for next week or next month when the rent is due, to just get the things done are not as important to my life, to my son's life, to my daughter's life and to my wife's life as will be that long range plan that looks ahead into the future. The long range plan looks beyond my children to my children's children. That is the way we should think.

When you are in business, you should not think of having a business just for your own immediate concerns. If you don't have children, you should think of other relatives and close friends. You should say: "I would like to see my relative or close friend inherit what I have. I hope to find one to qualify to take over this business before I leave this life." If that person is younger than you, that is good planning. We should work for the distant future and not just for today or the weekend. This will make our work more effective and long lasting and will make our work have more substance now and later.

Education, Business Training and Human Excellence

The Prophet said: "Live as though you are going to die tomorrow, but again live as though you are going to never die."

That means that your business should not be a seasonal business. If it is seasonal, then you should have a cycle of businesses. Say to yourself: "This business I am in is seasonal, and when its season runs out I will replace it with another one." Seasonal business does generate good money, although it may not last more than two weeks sometimes. But if you can see your success and hit it while it is hot, while opportunity is knocking at your door for a time, maybe only for two weeks, you may make good money. But don't stop there. Allah says: "As soon as you have finished or accomplished one beneficial task, immediately enter into another."

The common people, the people of small means who did not go to school to study business law and ethics and learn how to be decent and manage themselves also gain "establishment." They are just decent people by nature, by spirit and by habit. They will get into a business and thrive because of industriousness and decency. Allah will bless them to have that success. You may ask them: "How did you do all of that and you only have an eighth grade elementary school education?" They will answer: "Allah just blessed me." Or, "I've been fortunate. I can just put my hands to things and hopes materialize for me." You will meet people like that who have been very successful. I only think of how much more successful they would have been, if they had the education and business training or assistance to go with their natural excellence.

We have to understand that Allah tells us that He will not give the "Home of the Destiny" to anyone who desires a dominance. Now, how is that going to apply to small business? Perhaps the small business owner feels that he or she is not in a position or never will be in a position to even think of dominating Chicago or the United States or the world. However, the same attitude and the same disposition in those people who are in positions of power, in positions to have a dominance, may also be in you. You are not in touch with the whole world or for that matter the whole United States, but you are in touch with your life and with your world and with your immediate friends and customers. The Muslim believes that anyone who wants a dominance will not be successful. The Muslim believes it because Allah said it. If you have an attitude where you have to be above others all the time and have to have the controlling power all the time, and your desire to grow in business is for you to have more power over people, if you have an attitude requiring you to have others come look you up and you look no one up, then you are in this particular unfavorable picture.

There are many who are not even aware that they want to be more important in order to help spread corruption. There are many who want to be rich so they can help spread corruption and be in a situation to corrupt more people. This type of people just wants a whole lot of company in their corner of hell. Hell seems less of a hell when there is company. But the Muslim just remembers: "Bare and alone" is how the guilty will stand. If we are Muslims and we blindly have gotten into that greedy habit, then we should think on what Allah is saying to our attitudes. In this state of mind we should make an inspection of ourselves and be ready to reject what is not Muslim. Say to yourself: "This is not becoming of me. I am going to have to change this way of mine. I will check myself." The Qur'an helps us to check ourselves.

I believe two things generally account for success in business. The first is regard for something bigger and more important than self. The second is the ability to manage self. Big business and corporations are always giving seminars on their products and services, but they are also concentrating more on "personal" management than they are on other needs. The emphasis is on self, family, personal management. We know that the wife can make the husband a failure in business. We know that the husband can be responsible for making the wife a factor for his own failure and vice versa. This happens when he does not have a clear direction and a clear sense of what is demanded of him in the area of personal management.

If you are going to have a business, then you had better be able to manage your own appetites, your own passions. You cannot love a thing too much for your business. When you see yourself loving something too much for your business needs, then start to discipline your passions. Don't let passions destroy your business. You cannot hate too much for your business. A successful business person cannot be a bigot. How many bigots are successful in business? How many bigots do you think are running the material world? Most of the bigots are poor and angry because they are poor. Maybe they are bigots because they are poor.

The Qur'anic verse that I want to come back to now is the verse that most Muslim Imams and scholars refer to when they are bringing home the message that Muslims have no split or double life. That is, we have no life that is in moral conflict with itself. We do not have a life that is on one side open to religion and on the other side closed to religion. Our religion makes success in this world a range of merits for greater life in the next. Muslims do not believe that the material world is to be the domain of Satan. We do not believe that material is evil of itself. We do not believe that raw (uneducated) nature is evil of itself.

were not necessary to be placed in the Qur'an. They were issues that the common man could address with common sense. The Prophet addressed common sense issues and the Prophet is the most excellent common sense man Allah made. He was the most excellent behaving man before he was called to carry the word of Allah. Muhammed the Messenger of Allah was complete as concerns the whole range of possibilities opened to man by Allah. The range would include life in the home and life in the public, life in business and life in government, life in the military and life as the chief executive. As a private citizen, as a private man in the home with a wife and children, Muhammed proved and demonstrated that excellence. Muhammed taught the total life and how to live it, so that we benefit by our full potential.

Al-lslam offers people an opportunity to get rid of the identity problem mothered by racism. "Islam" gets rid of that right away. We find a more meaningful sense of pride and dignity upon accepting the Muslim life with its behavior mold and established precious values. Al-lslam was before the United States. The best citizens of the United States are those who have a way of life of their choice ruling over their behavior. Such people live in worlds bigger than geographical boundaries. Those nations are stronger and better preserved that are blessed to have such citizens in large numbers. It is a good feeling knowing you belong to those precious numbers. As a Muslim, my life is before this world in the dimensions of time and my Muslim life survives to outlive pop cultures and can outlive nations.

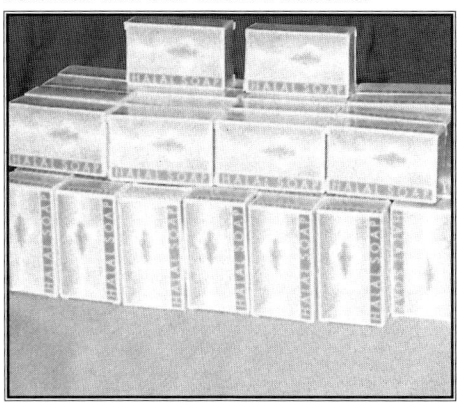

During the Muslim Owners Business Conference, Muslim businessmen and business women who came to Newark, N.J., from across the United States that May 27-28, 1995, weekend stressed the economic value in Muslims buying from Muslims - even the simplest of items, like this "Halal Soap" on sale by one of the Muslim vendors. The point was made that every Muslim uses soap!

ISLAM'S CLIMATE FOR BUSINESS SUCCESS

The African American Contractors Association, based in Chicago, Illinois, chose as one of its honorees for 1995, Imam W. Deen Mohammed, who addressed the Association, March 22, 1995.

(R-L) Bro. Omar Shareef, President of the African American Contractors Association and founder of Universal Construction Services, shares a moment with Imam W. Deen Mohammed at the A.A.C.A.'s Award Reception. Tayyab, the son of Omar Shareef, is also a regular at business meetings and affairs accompanying his father.

Priorities For An Advancing People

As for our priorities, first of all, we want good relationships with all people. America is a country of many people, "E Pluribus Unum" - "out of many, one." It is not only many people from different nations, but we are also many ethnic groups in one big culture called America. We are many ethnic aspirations in one big aspiration called America. But I don't see my permanence in America. I see my permanence with Allah. No Christian should see their permanence in America; you should see your permanence with God. No Jew or anyone else should see their permanence in America; their permanence should be with God.

I depend on my Islamic life more than I depend on my American life. A Jew should depend on his Jewish life more than he depends on his American life. It is because our religious life is protected by God, if we are sincere. America will not always be protected by God, if we leave that which God loves, that which God cherishes. God loves our obedience to Him. God loves that we want to follow the Path that He set for us. If we leave that, we will not exist here very long as comfortable and secure American citizens.

What makes this country so great is that it invites people from various backgrounds and various religions to come here and live their religions without fearing persecution. We were persecuted before. Frederick Douglass and Sojourner Truth - as they were able to press forward, so are we. There is a slave who is almost insignificant in our history called Julia. She said a powerful thing; it was so powerful a White man had to record it. She said: "You look like God in the face and act like the devil in your hearts." We owe a lot to courageous people like Julia.

If we want a better life for ourselves separately as Muslims or Christians or whatever we are in America, we as a people had better be able to identify what is the basis and where are the grounds for our unity. Where do we locate the real force that has been driving us to more and more excellence and to more and more courage to defend what is right and to condemn what is wrong? To go into the open door of opportunity, even if someone says you are going to be killed when you step in there? Something says, "Die for your dignity. Die for your God-given humanity." We don't want anything defected, weak and small in value.

Doing For Self

Because I am not believing in the theology of the Nation of Islam that we were in before should not make anyone come to the conclusion that I don't like "doing for self." No one should come to the conclusion that I don't like seeing us work for business establishment and economic empowerment. What would make anyone think that I am not for that, when I am as busy as I am with shahadah (declaring faith), salat (prayer), zakat (charity), siyam (fasting), Hajj (pilgrimage to Mecca) and the principles of Faith: Belief in God, in His Angels, in His Messengers, in His Books, in Judgement Day, in the Life Hereafter, and in the Law of God that Rewards and Punishes?

I believe in all of Islam. What in my behavior would make anyone think that I don't want money any more or don't want business any more or that I am not for our people coming out of their poor showing in business and into a better showing? We want establishment in America. We want establishment that we don't have to be ashamed of. I feel proud of African Americans in the media and in the business corporate world who make big money. However, there is not nearly enough of them. We are fastly traveling out of inferiority into excellence and strength. This is what we want. We want to get into situations where we can use our resources and improve our skills and become resourceful enough to produce for ourselves, so the White man won't have to carry us. We have to carry ourselves.

We have African Americans, men and women, who have risen up into the political life of America and into governmental, educational and business systems and are now able to do much for their people, which was done before only by Whites. I feel good about that and want to see us be more responsible for education in our own communities and in our own cities. We should support an independent effort. It is known that I support us doing this within the system - working as teachers and as principals and as superintendents in the school system. And I also want to see a separate and independent effort. I am a supporter of the United Negro College Fund; I am a supporter of what it stands for. I give of myself, to the excellence and longevity of our own investments in our own life and its future.

We as Muslim African Americans, are really growing now in a way that I think should make all of us feel comfortable. When you can have a jumuah in Atlanta and eight hundred or more people attend that jumuah, I think we the Muslims should feel very good about that all over these United States. That means that we have now recovered from a set back. Not only have we recovered from a set back, but now we have been renewed. Sometimes you may recover and after recovery you will be where you were before. But we are recovered and renewed. I do not think it would have been possible to get this great spirit we are witnessing today from a recovery that does not amount to a renewal. Many of the brothers and sisters are not situated mentally and emotionally to cooperate and to stand by their commitment.

This new and growing activity in certain cities makes me feel like we have regained our spirit to achieve, to be producers. Many of us did not lose it, but the majority did and worked to kill the atmosphere for everybody. Now recovering, we are a new people, and Allah is with us. I would like you to know in my own way, with my own intelligence and ability and feeling for what is right, that I have promoted those aspirations and concerns necessary for a people wanting strength and production. We want strong people. We don't want to be weak people. We want stability. We don't want people here today and gone tomorrow. In order to have people who can hold to their Muslim way of life and pass on what they have to their children (inheritors), we have to make sound investments in the future.

We make an investment in the future for the soul by obeying Allah. Obeying our Lord Allah is the first investment and the most important investment. Obey Allah so that we will have a future on earth and in the Hereafter. That is the investment. But we have to be aware that Allah requires of us that we be a people respected by others for our contribution to today's needs and tomorrow's needs. We are to build for this generation and the generations to come. Allah wants us to invest in the future. We have to invest materially for improved education, strong schools and strong business. We cannot depend on one-profession preachers and propagators to establish a community. Preachers and propagators can only attract and call people to the Word of Allah. Once people are called to the Word (the Qur'an) of Allah, then the people have to understand their obligation as believers.

If we are believers in the Word of Allah, we are obligated to make good use of everything that Allah offers the believer. If you have time and don't spend it well, Allah will hold you accountable. If you have money and don't spend it well, Allah will hold you accountable. If you have knowledge and don't spend it well, Allah will hold you accountable. We believe Allah will hold us accountable for what we are doing with our resources. If we have only resources of the heart and no resources of the brain, then we are not whole Muslims. We will not be crippled and handicapped Muslims, for we are to have resources of the heart and also resources of the brain. If we do not have living conditions to influence people to have respect for us, we are still coming up short. Muslims have to have living conditions that get them respect. We want all Muslims making investments for the future - investments for schools and education and business. If you work on education and business, you will not have to walk with your head down.

We could make money the crooked way, which is quick and easy. I do not know about other nationalities, but all the crooks in the African American community collect money for the dominant race. In our case it is the Whites who eventually get it all. So even if I were not a Muslim or a believer in right actions, being a "Black" criminal would not be attractive to me.

Allah compares life and resurrection of an individual with life and resurrection of a town. Allah gives us that parable in the Qur'an. Allah points us to a town all dilapidated and neglected and in need of a resurrection. We want to resurrect towns and start with our own. We welcome a time when there are enough successful people in Robbins, Illinois, to guarantee there will be no problem of poverty.

The Working Poor

Zakat is for the needy and the poor. From people (poor) in your same situation there is no obligation to the idle and lazy poor who want zakat. Most of our supporters are people who are poor but they give zakat. These poor people want to help pay the rent and the lights for the masjid. They want to help the school. They want to help propagation. What justification is there for us to take from a brother who has no more education than this other brother, and has no more physical ability than this other brother, and works for a living; what justification do we have to give this poor working brother's money to the lazy poor? This poor working brother will not accept that there is no work. He will go and find work. He will get a bucket and a rag and will ask people can he wash their car. He comes back and gives to charities. He will eat a little, spend a little and will put something in zakat. What right do we have to take from that brother and give it to another brother who will not work for a living?

The industrious poor brother will have children that he is taking care of. But the other (lazy) brother has children and is not taking care of them and he is not loyal to any, but he wants zakat. That brother needs to be (morally) redeemed first. As long as we are a poor community, we have to see all of our people as poor. We African-American people are a poor people. We have some people who are doing well and we know that, but group-wise we are poor. No matter how well some of us are doing, as a people we are mostly idle and poor. Until that changes, I will be protecting the poor from the poor. What my ministry receives in charity is mostly coming from poor people. I have an obligation to spend as those contributors want me to spend. They did not give their zakat to the lazy. These believers (Muslims) are trusting that their Imam will not take care of lazy people with their money they have sacrificed. If they (who give charity) wanted to help the idle and lazy, they have too many like that all around them. They do not have to send money for that. I do not mean to disrespect any of you in your *dignified* poverty.

Imams, do not be satisfied receiving no income except from charity. If you want more education and think that you need to go back to school, you should do that. We have helped some Imams and they have done well. We have helped some brothers and sisters who are not Imams. We are all helped when some of us achieve more. Some of you Imams are doing well in education, business and other professions. We have to make sure that what we have is spent to get the best results for our overall interest. So we spend on people who show by their example they are really honest and hard working and are really going to make a contribution if they can get the needed assistance.

Our successful business people should help us inform our brothers and sisters to improve their eligibility for financial assistance. We are not in the business of taking people who have nothing materially and putting them into some materially good situation. We can't do that, and that never will be the masjid's role. The masjid's role is only to address the needs in our spirit and the needs in our thinking. We call people to a disposition within (ourselves) that will mean success in this life and in the Hereafter. The obligation on the Imam is to address the spirit and the thinking. "You will not believe until your inclinations follow what I have come with." (Muhammed the Last Prophet)

I would like to see us grow with more appreciation for this religion as the religion of successful people. Allah says: "...and the believers must win through." The believers must triumph because what they believe in is productive. This is what we have been missing. We have been misdirected and made afraid to talk about investing for achievement. We want achievement, and we want a continuous life. Allah, the Merciful, says to the Prophet: "When you finish one thing, get involved productively in something else." When we finish one thing, don't accept to be idle.

Allah has given us opportunity and has provided the necessary resources. What will be done with opportunities depends on conditions within and also the circumstances without or outside of our persons. Sometimes the circumstances without are good, but the conditions within are bad. Therefore, we cannot get the benefit. Sometimes the conditions within are good and the circumstances without are bad and we can't get the benefit. Once conditions are right within, maybe we will be stopped today, but we will never accept to be quitters. I am glad that I was born into the environment where people had faith in themselves. My father and my mother were hard working sacrificing country folks who did not believe in lying around vegetating and turning into dust. My parents did not accept to be idle. They believed that they could make it.

I heard my mother, Clara Muhammad, say: "Well, I don't know how long we will have what we've got. But I know that I can get out here, if I have to, and wash and iron and take care of other people's clothes." My mother was not going to accept that she was going to sit some where and die because no one would give her something. She would say, "I know I can make it." And that spirit went into us. My father, the Hon. Elijah Muhammad - I do not have to tell you about him. Everyone knows him. He told us to "do for self." I am never ready to quit, but I am patient. I want to be very patient. I like to see where I'm going. I don't like to move in the dark.

I am aware, however, that being slow or procrastinating or putting off till tomorrow what I should be doing today is a problem and a defect. Yet, I do not move too fast in certain situations.

We will raise ourselves up by our own work efforts and by our obedience to Allah. Steadily we will rise up out of poverty and out of the image of a people complaining and begging. Our spirit will not let us be a people depending on others for our tomorrows. I don't want you to get lost in material mindedness, but Allah has inspired me, I do believe, to work for righteous establishment, for strong business, for those strong institutions needed in community life. We want to be a strong industrious people who can make and sustain material accomplishments in this life. We must keep in mind all is made possible by Merciful Allah.

Isn't it wonderful to see as a part of religion the material accomplishments. All Allah asks is for us to keep the Taqwa - keep the fear and obedience to Him. Those who have accomplishments will be over those who have no accomplishments. Those who have material achievements will be over those who have no material achievements. We don't want to be slaves to people of material means. Malcolm X had a way of dealing with the White man when the White man would be tightening the screws on him. Malcolm would say, "Why don't you just ask yourself what do you want?" He would then say, "Well, that is what I want." Now I will add, "And we want it halal!" That is to say, we want only what is lawful.

I am sure that all of us are aware of the burden on us as a people (racially). No matter how successful we are individually, I am sure all of us are aware of the image given "Blacks". That we waste our resources. That we fear to invest. That we are inclined to gamble more so than to use our intelligence and good logic to plan for a successful life. That we will give our money to riskful situations. The Muslim African American (Blacks) must accept the Muslims' responsibility to work for the life of the Hereafter and also for the life here and now. Don't be afraid to invest. We are not going to always be successful. But, sincerely believing in Allah, we see an investment that is proper for Muslims according to our intelligence and we should not be afraid. If we fail, we try and try again. We will never give up, and never accept that we are not responsible.

Make calculated moves with knowledge. Get knowledge of the situation before you invest. Be sure that you have researched and studied the matter. Then go on and have the courage to invest. Success belongs to the people who have that courage. If you invest nothing, then you get nothing. Isn't that common sense, and isn't that what we have been told? If you put nothing in, then you get nothing out. Some of us cannot even be farmers anymore. We are afraid that the seed won't come up. Our fathers and mothers had the faith to plant. They would plant and expect a harvest and worked for a harvest. We are to be as they were. Invest something into the world in order to get something out of the world.

If you are not in a position to invest, then work at getting yourself into a position to make an investment. What is it that Allah tells us over and over again in the Qur'an? It is "to spend." Do you know what that means most of the time? It means to invest. It is to invest today for the good tomorrow. But do it loving Allah and obeying Him. Thus situated, Allah assures us that we will be successful. Those who study the financial situation of the African American as a people are saying we are great consumers and spenders. By force of habit we give our resources and best opportunities to other people. We make other people rich and our race poor, dependent.

It is a common error to think that our Prophet Muhammed had no wealth. Our Prophet (PBUH) was no poor man. Even before he was missioned the Prophet, he was a businessman working in the employment of Lady Khadijah, the mother of the Faithful, may Allah be pleased with her. He was such great assistance to her and to her business, that she put him over her business. He was successful at what he did. We should know that our Prophet was a successful business person. They say the Prophet did not have any money because he slept on a little thin mat. But many of us would benefit by such discipline. When we rise and begin our day, will we care to ask, "What is the financial situation of the good believers? Come, we want to improve it. Take this sum from today's balance and go and invest it. Help the community." Prophet Muhammed had so much given to him and trusted to him that he just passed it out to bright, good minded and industrious people. He gave great wealth to the needs of individuals and the society. That generous giving was the Prophet's investments.

I have to follow my Prophet all the way, if my spirit is to be satisfied. One day I see myself saying: "Tell them I want to invest in the transportation business, privately owned railroad trains and commercial airplanes." I would like to see that day when I can say: "How many employees do we have in that new bank? We have more money than is needed to operate. There are no attractive investments for our consideration. Therefore, we will invest directly in more employment. Build another facility to train and educate more employees for success in the banking field." We should know how holy and righteous business can be. All you need to do is have your hearts in the right place. Have your hearts with Allah. Accept the guidance of the Qur'an and the life example of our Prophet and go after what is needed to establish yourselves, not only spiritually but also materially.

The business of dawah (propagation and education) is also a prominent part of the Ministry of Imam W. Deen Mohammed through "W. Deen Mohammed Publications."

The Muslim Journal - a Muslim business in operation since 1975 through its Exhibit in Washington, D.C., at the 1994 Annual Islamic Convention, brought to view the many milestones established and others reached by this Muslim community.

67

Prepared To Make It In The Land of Plenty

The world is loaded with goods and delights. There is a saying of the Prophet, the peace and the blessings be upon him, about Allah's creation and the change that took place in that creation. The saying goes that Allah invited the Great Angel Jibril to witness His creation. And when Jibril beheld the creation of Allah, he said: "How can anyone go wrong in this creation?" Allah then showed the Great Angel Jibril His creation after Satan had altered it. Then Jibril said: "Oh my Lord, how can anyone go straight in this creation?" So we live in a world created by Allah but altered by the enemy. We live in a world of natural creation and artificial creation or artificiality. We live in Allah's creation and also in man's creation. Man's creation is not always good for us, as we know. There are issues now about the environment and so many other issues that are very important because of man making mistakes in his works. Sometimes he has been careless in his works and in not considering the good environmental future of humanity.

The world is sensible and foolish. The world is both decent and indecent. The world is kind and cruel. The world is peacemaker and peace-breaker. Though the world must accommodate honesty and work to preserve honesty and cannot live without honesty, the world is both honest and deceitful. The world is not incapable of converting its every utility, charity and blessings into instruments of war: War for control.

America stands out among the nations in the most peculiar character of all nations. As I see it, it is the most dangerous land. Nevertheless, if you are strong and decent, the mighty arm of the world will not break you. But understand that you have to be prepared to make it in the land of plenty. There is a need to keep an eye on what you want from yourself and an eye on what you want from America. Many of us do not give any serious thought to what we want from ourselves. And that is the big mistake.

Muslims or religious people are influenced by the religion to keep an eye on self, and to present "self" at all times in a way that would please our Lord and Maker, Allah. We are believing that we have to always present ourselves in a way that permits us to be in a good situation for progress in the land of plenty.

Since our disposition and attitude have a way of telling what we are prepared for, it makes good sense then to be prepared within, internally. I remember my father, the late leader, once saying to the great gathering of his people: "I see how beautiful you are dressed without. But how are you dressed within?" It is in spiritual expression where we can observe the force of sensitivities maximized, concentrated and directed. Religion wants us to come into the proper spirit, into that spirit which Allah intended for His human creation.

Question a person's morals, passions, or intelligence, and a spirit may take control of that person. As situations grow around us and in us, as in the affluent society we call America, those situations become more serious, more complex, less simple for us to manage. The more complex and serious the situation becomes around us and within us, the more we have to sharpen our senses and sensitivities. By the expression "sharpened sensitivities" is meant we must have more "experienced sensitivities." Many people live long lives but never have matured sensitivities. Those sensitivities do not seem to improve much over the period of their experiences. That is because they are people who are absent-minded or people who have no real cares. As Allah says to us, He has given us signs in the heavens and in the earth as well as in ourselves, but most go on heedless and unaware. By sharpened sensitivities is meant disciplined sensitivities. Experience permits us to come into disciplines.

I was watching a program on television where an instructor in music was praising her young student who showed exceptional ability at an awards program. This teacher said of that great ability that was demonstrated by this youngster: "All I did was channel the natural instincts that were created by God." What we want to understand is that Allah put our treasures into our nature to meet the demands from without. No matter what our present situation is, we are all created with the same excellence. However, that excellence has to have a condition and circumstances for its coming forth.

Just as the plant has to have the condition and circumstances for its coming forth from the earth from a dead seed, the human being has to have the climate for success. It is called a "dead seed," but is the seed really dead? The seed is not dead as a stone is dead. You can put a stone in the earth, and the rains will come and the warmth will come and the circumstances will come, but nothing will happen. But if you put a seed in the earth which appears to be as dead as a stone - and many seeds are called stones - something happens when the circumstances come. The seed swells and grows into a beautiful plant and a useful thing. Likewise, it is for us. A parable of the human life in all its descriptions is plant life with all of its descriptions (Qur'an).

Value Our Human Creation For Success

We have to value our own creation to make it in the land of plenty. Many of the failing people in the land of plenty have no real appreciation for what they are naturally in their creation. They are fascinated and distracted so much so that they just follow "shadows that are cast by things that they cannot even identify." They will just follow influences in the confused atmosphere of degenerated cultural life. They follow those influences and will take their minds and personalities and behavior from those influences of the confused culture around them. So how can they make it in the land of plenty? It is impossible to make it in the land of plenty with that weakness in them.

We are especially happy and excited about the fact that we have come into Al-lslam and that we are Muslims. That is, we believe we have a situation for our life that is good. I made a trip to mainland China with a group of Americans as Friends of China and America, as friends of both people. When we arrived there we were met by a Chinese host and finally were taken to the one who was to address us. He began his introduction saying: "The situation is good in the heavens." Well, I feel as a Muslim that the situations are good now on earth. I don't know if I understood what he meant by saying the situation was good in the heavens, because I used to believe that the situation was always good in the heavens. The heavens were set by Allah. My heart was always content in heaven, but now I also feel the situation is good on earth.

Not only do I realize that I have a good religion - not only do I realize that I have a religion that can please humanity - I have a religion that can answer all of the needs of men of my color or of any other color. I have a religion that can accommodate my greatest desires and my greatest aspirations. I have a religion that can open doors for me that I see and doors I have not yet seen. That is why I feel so wonderful. Having faith in religion and faith in my creation, I will say with all of my heart and spirit, "the situation is good on earth."

Returning to the need for disciplined sensitivities, through experience they become more fit and better prepared to survive moral, social, financial, and political confusion in the land of plenty. We are going to have plenty moral confusion, social confusion, financial confusion and political confusion in the land of plenty. If we were in a small country and were to go to some of the beautiful resort places for tourists in the Caribbean areas or to Morocco, there we do not have the same situation. In less industrialized areas we are not threatened so much by moral confusion, social confusion, financial confusion and by typical big city problems.

Overly played up moral concerns have reduced the likelihood of us making it in the land of plenty. "We can't be too moral!" In our religion the rule is to guard against the extremes, because the extremes are bad. The extremes spoil a thing. The extremes will take a good thing out of its true nature. When you go to moral extremes, to a certain point or degree where you are over playing moral life, then you have taken the moral life out of its true nature. Therefore, we have to be careful not to go after moral extremes to the extent that we over play the importance of morality.

We have perhaps known some self righteous prudes down

here on earth. They are not in heaven, but want us to think they are. Some want to be called holy. They will go to sleep on their feet while soaking up this praise. Some will hold their heads high because they think they have a moral spirit above what is human excellence. What they have is moral arrogance. We must be aware of moral exaggerations. Moral excellence cannot be established without a situation for a functional life of morals and intelligence. We have to have those two working together.

Allah says that if the earth had been populated by angels, then He "would have sent an angel as a messenger." This is not to criticize or reject angels, for we know that angles are high in the creation of Allah. But Allah has de-emphasized the exaggerated attention that religious societies gave angelic behavior prior to the advent of our Prophet Muhammed. In some respects, some religious representatives are saying to become angels without our human nature is our highest goal. What I am saying is the goal for us is to become human and obedient like the angels, but don't become like the angels and turn away from the wife and husband. Don't say: "Well we can be friends but no more intimate relations, for I'm too holy for that!" Don't become angels and operate in the dark; man is made with eyes to see by the light and to progress upon a study of the light.

We want to pursue our human destiny, and the human destiny is to be functional in this world. It is to be functional for the good of humanity, itself. Allah says of the Muslim community that you are the best community evolved for what? Allah says it: "...evolved for the benefit of all people." And the Prophet, the peace and the blessings be upon him, said: "And the best of you is the one who benefits the people."

Benefits For Humanity

We know that in the history of civilization and in the history of civilizers, we can find no one who has come with the benefits for humanity equal to that which our Prophet brought, peace and the blessings be upon Muhammed. We are not the only ones with this excitement and appreciation for his great successes. Western writers also say there is no one else in history who came and did so much in such a short span of time and had so little to work with. The Prophet came to a backward people, a people during the Dark Ages who were as backward or even more backward than any other people at that time. They were the people called "jahiliyyah of Arabia."

The Prophet came with the message of Al-Islam, with the Qur'an, and with the excellence that Allah created him to be. And it was the revelation and the Prophet that transformed that backward society, and Arabia was brought up to be the brilliant jewel of this earth in a time of ignorance, savagery, and in a time of all kinds of abuses of human life. We know what religion can do. We have it in history. We have a clear history of the successes and power of religion. And we are happy to be in this religion and to invite those who are not in it to examine the Qur'an and to study.

We are not demagogues. We are not a people who will deprive you of your freedom of thought. Muslims do not ask anyone to believe because we believe. We want you to believe because you have used your good intelligence and your good virtues and you have looked at its worth for yourself. You have decided upon the test of your virtues and upon the test of your good intelligence that this is the virtuous religion and this is the intelligent religion that you would like.

Whatever we do should testify to the glory and greatness of Allah. Isn't that what the Christian hymn says: "Praise God with your life. Praise God with everything you do." We have to appreciate working for the pleasure of Allah. When you work for the pleasure of Allah, you are working for the maximum good for self and others. Now what makes us sometimes ineffective? You will say, "I don't see any results." The reason is we are not prepared to get the results. We have Muslims among us who have never been satisfied with their preparedness. They always want to become better prepared. Always make an effort or at least desire better for yourself with the next opportunity. If it is for something real, do not lose the desire; nourish the desire and love the desire. And in time, "the virtual power of the desire" itself will bring about the action. Prepare to do better.

Our society in the land of plenty does not honorably value children and parents. How can obedience be expected of children, when parents are discredited? When all of the principle of respect and credit is taken away from parents? It seems to be an international effort to break the respectful bond which holds parents and children together in a natural, working (socially functioning) relationship. The establishment will address the children on matters as though the children are grown and independent. From positions on the school campuses and on the television, they will be speaking to youngsters and telling youngsters that they have to do something to protect themselves. "You have to buy condoms. You have to get sex education." The establishment has gone so far as to push children to disobey parents' wishes.

I have witnessed the establishment changing the behavioral spirit of children by telling them, "If your parents deny you something or speak harshly to you - they do not have to beat you physically, but if they are guilty of just verbal abuse, you can report them to the law." That is not the way to solve America's social problems. You must have a meeting with parents first. You must try to educate parents first. And if you can't educate parents, and those parents defy your every attempt, then you tell those parents: "Now we are going to tell the children that we respected their parents and asked them to address sex behavior in order to save children for graduations and for happy marriages." But even at this sad stage in the matter, still respect the parents and tell them: "We are going to do the best we can to keep the respect. We will word our language in the best way we possibly can." There are always enough heedful parents in cities to answer a call by the establishment requesting that parents form a parents' front for calling the children of the city to accept the meaning of sex in the social establishment context.

Our religion teaches us: "Never go in by the back door. Go in by the front door." Never call on the house and not address the adults. You must address the adults. Members of the public do not speak to children when the adults are away. You have to respect the adults of the house. This is what our society has not done. Too many Americans have lost the good sense of respect for established values. Allah established the way when He created us; creation treasures Allah's way. Also the children are to be respected. Our religion does not leave us without proper regard for children. Religion, however, also stresses obedience in children for their parents.

Allah, Most High, says in the Qur'an: "If your parents contend with you to get you to associate with Allah that which has not any support in knowledge, do not obey them but keep good relationships with them in this world." Our religion is considerate and rational. Before us is Allah, the Lord of the Worlds, addressing us. How many of us in our positions of authority and power of leadership could say: "Child, if your parents do not accept my leadership, then don't follow them in that, but still keep good relations with them." Most with power and leadership, if the child comes to them and says: "My parents say that you are to be rejected" - their response would be: "Arm yourself against your parents." Isn't that typical of revolutions?

The Climate of Tolerance and Balanced Revolution

Muslims have a revolution. Al-lslam is a revolution. It is the most civilized revolution. We are not asked to go out and kill parents and fight parents because they tell their children to reject Al-lslam. Allah says, "Don't obey parents in false worship, but keep good relationships with them in this world." Muslims are to be peacemakers. "Be not aggressors." And, "If those who fight you incline toward peace, incline yourselves also." (Qur'an) People attacked our religion. People attacked Prophet Muhammed, peace and blessings be upon the Prophet. Peace and blessings be upon the Christ-Prophet Jesus, they called Jesus and others "mad". The Prophets did not come out and say, "Kill them!"

Meccans persecuted, boycotted and caused Prophet Muhammed to leave Mecca, his hometown. When the Prophet was able to really kill his enemies, he announced a period of forgiveness and said: "All offenses of the past are forgiven." There

I have studied some works of anthropologists and sociologists, like Margaret Mead, who studied primitive societies. And some have come to the conclusion that human excellence can best be observed in primitive society. We can look at the Pygmies and still be in line with our concern on personal management. A study of the Pygmies found a high moral sense and a high moral code. It was found that Pygmies did not steal from each other. They did not abuse each other; there was no physical abuse cases among them. There was great respect for their children and great respect from children for parents. They had strong, morally bonded families. But they did not have modern civilization, technology, asphalt and concrete, or a modern jungle. This is not to invite us to turn our backs on civilization, for we cannot do that. But this is to say: Go back in the road and pick up the humanity that we have been separated from and bring it up with our advances.

Allah says: *"And seek with whatever means He has availed you the Home of the Destiny, but do not forget your share of this world."* I hear it! Allah is saying to me: "Wallace, do not forget your share of Chicago. And if you move to Bridgeport, don't forget your share of Bridgeport. You have a citizenship in the United States, so do not forget your share of the United States. Do not forget your share of Planet Earth." Some now may think that I am being a little materialistic. While others thought that I couldn't do anything but float. Neither is the case, for I keep hearing what Allah has said. It rings clearer and clearer, and I am tired of not having my share. I have some associates with me now who have business minds as well as spiritual minds, and we are really working on getting our share. Moreover, when we get our share, we are not going to forget that Allah says: "The Home of the Destiny is best and more gratifying."

Our business plan must include a plan for charity, as well as a plan for free and low-cost service to business persons wanting business life and strong establishment. We hope to be in a position one day to help business people who qualify. We know the system and the law is pretty straight, but too many of the people are still pretty crooked and I am referring to all races of American people. It can be the African-American attorney, the European-

American, or the Asian-American businessman. It may also be the financial institution given to unethical practices. The law will be good, but the person no good. They might be strategically placed in the business for the purpose of stopping people like us.

Then there are some who think we should have a campaign to just preach love for others. "Love your White brother, Blackman. Love your Black brother, Whiteman. This world has too much hate." But sometimes ignoring a person works better. If you really know they hate you, then you should not care for their love. Even if 80 percent of the American people were to hate me, I would not want their love. I would be satisfied with the 20 percent who feel about me the way I feel about them. That 80 percent I would ignore; I would not be out trying to win their love by appealing to their capacity to give love or to their capacity to receive love. Although, I would not ignore them completely; I would be conscious of the danger or the threat to me from them. But I do not care for love with race haters. All you can do is keep a comfortable distance between them and you. That is the way to win their love, if there is any to be won.

Regard for a Higher Power - Managing Self and Family

Understand that the most important day in the life of a Muslim is Friday, the Day of Jumuah. The Prophet, peace and blessings be upon him, has said: "It is the day on which Adam was created and the day on which he ascended." The Prophet also said that no one is resurrected on any other day but Friday; it is the day for our resurrection. It is the only day of the week that a lecture is given along with midday congregational prayer. Otherwise, this is done only for the Muslim observance days (holidays). Allah says for that day: "When you have responded to the call to come to Jumuah, then disperse back into the avenues of business and profit." Allah did not say: "Remember this is Friday, the day of rest. Go home and have dinner and listen to hymns." Allah said that after Jumuah: "Then disperse back into the avenues of the industrious people."

"Disperse" means that all of us should not have hamburger joints, all of us should not have fried fish houses. Allah said "disperse," which means the people who are leaving have to have varied kinds of business interests and involvements. The businesses have to be different in order for them to disperse. Disperse means to go out in all directions. One will be going back to building a house. The other will be going back to farming the land. Another will be going back to work in the hospital. There will be the shoemaker and the transportation serviceman. A Muslim business directory should be a good reflection of the business life of the whole city or town. Allah wants us to be aware of the many needs and services that man has, to be conscious and try to supply needs.

The United States is a country that encourages desire in its citizens for diversified business establishments. Regretfully, a desire to "get over quick" is working against our neighborhoods. "Do you know Brother Shaheed? He has a fish store on Vine Street, and it is really going! I'm going to put me one down there." We should know that competition is good, but "throat cutting" is not what Allah wants. Going to Vine Street may bring Brother Shaheed more fish customers. A business person will not succeed whose values are too low, whose interests are too narrow and weak.

Islam as a religion addresses the needs of the total person. In the view of the scholars and students, Al-lslam is a comprehensive religion. That means that this religion takes into its focus every aspect of the life and all of the needs for that life. It is not just for one person in their narrow world. The language of this religion, Al-lslam, is respecting and giving recognition to business in a classic way. The Qur'an, itself, promotes good business sense. It tells the reader that if you are successful in anything that brings you income and property, then you should be careful "not" to pass on the responsibility for that concern that you have worked hard to establish to a person who is not qualified to keep it up and take care of it as you would. This even applies to the person you might want to put in that position, even if it is your own child. This is the advice in Qur'an for the business person and for the property owner: "Do not give (business) responsibility to the feeble-minded."

The Qur'anic term that is translated as "feeble-minded" is not referring to a mentally retarded individual. The language and the context make it very clear to us that it means a person who is undisciplined and does not have the business interest to value and respect the responsibility, if it were trusted to him. The person you trust your property or business to should have the appreciation for it to take it into their hands and manage it as well as or better than you would. Pass your works on to the person who is sharp minded and values your work as you value it.

The effect that I want when I conclude is for you who identify as Muslims and as business people to feel a closer relationship to the Word of Allah in the Qur'an. I want you to feel that when you have the Qur'an, you have a partner with you in business. You don't have to go to a psychologist and pay a huge fee in order to get your spirit up and to start thinking positive and to get the energy to go back to work. All you have to do is consult the pages of the Qur'an. I'll also tell you what to look for. Look for that verse that says: "Do not neglect your share of this world." That is Allah, the Creator and Lord Most High, talking. Before I read that in Qur'an, I remembered my parents told me the same thing, but not in those words. They said: "Son, make something of yourself and don't die poor." My mother had known mean poverty. And I do not blame anyone who knew poverty and still have their good senses for telling their children, "Don't die poor." All of us should look at a child in the morning and first say: "As-Salaam-Alaikum, and don't die poor!" That is, be Muslim, be peace loving believers but don't die in poverty without having worked to establish yourself.

The Qur'an also tells us that we should make wills. We know we are going to die, so do not die without leaving a will or a legal trust. The Qur'an even tells us how to make the will. Males in the family are to get a bigger share than the females. Some will say: "That's not fair." But you have to also look at the state of our men today. If I could change the Word of Allah, and I have no desire to do that, I would say: "The boys are to get four-fifths." I would increase it. If I asked: "How many sisters here are employed," I know you would see more hands go up than brothers', if brothers were asked the same. Even those sisters who list themselves as home keepers and housewives, they are employed and have full time jobs. So brothers, it looks like African-American men are the main ones with a problem of unemployment. No matter what has happened in the work place to give women equality, still the burden is on the males. And no one yet has excused men from that responsibility. "African-American man, why don't you take care of your wife? It is not her responsibility to take care of those children." We men cannot say: "This is equality of the sexes now." No one is going to pay any attention to that answer.

It looks like nature is overruling much of this one-sidedness. The woman is asking: "Can I drive the mail truck?" And we will tell her: "Yes, baby take it." Then she will come back home and look at herself in the mirror, and pretty soon she is so angry she'll say: "African-American man, you have to go. I don't need you!" Now, I believe in equality, but it must be equality based on reality. The sister has the same intellect, the same morality, but unless something happens to change things, she does not have the same physique or physiology. She does not have the same spirit for going out and chopping down trees and breaking concrete and hauling iron and driving a truck all night. The physiology of a woman will change if she takes on these roles. If she drives a truck all the time, she will go out from the waist into a bulky and awkward spread at the bottom.

The Holy Qur'an speaks on inheritance in this way. The female has a right to inheritance and the male has a right to inheritance. The Holy Qur'an tells us that men have a right to go into business and women have a right to go into business. But again, it also tells us that the burden of maintaining a family is on the male. If the female is in a good financial situation, it is her right to say: "Honey, I have money. Use this money. You need a new car. You need a new suit. Let me pay this bill, so you can get yourself a new suit. You have worked hard all week." However, according to Allah's guidance, even if the wife has $50,000 in the bank and no demands are on the family at the time, and I, as her husband, may make $5 an hour or less; still I have no right to tell her: "We are to share your wealth equally. You have the money, and I'm not making more than $200 a week. So you pay the electric bill and the rent this month." That is not right.

If a man makes the big mistake of marrying a woman who is much superior to him, then he will just have to suffer for his mistake. According to our religion, I cannot make any demands on my wife's money. If she wants to give something of her own free will, if she wishes to buy me a milk shake, then that is her business. I should say, "Thank you, Sweetheart!" For Allah has not changed His Guidance; He says that we men are the maintainers of the women. Men are the ones who are supposed to bring that money in and take care of the rent, the utilities and give wives and children their due. It is painful to have one's wife looking at him producing nothing but children and the bills are never caught up.

Yet some men will pop the surprise and tell a wife: "I want you to meet Sister Sultana, and I want to make her my second wife." Now we know there are Islamic grounds for polygamy, where you can have more than one wife with four being the limit. But if you are reading the Holy Qur'an, we know also that you cannot have a second wife without regard for the financial qualifications. When a man marries a second wife, he should be marrying her because he has the material means and financial strength to take care of more. If he is not meeting his responsibilities now, how does he look asking for a second wife? Some will say: "Sister, I would like to have a second wife." Now when a brother starts calling his wife "sister," look out! He will start stammering in Arabic: "Sister, I will show you here in the Qur'an. You mean you are telling me that I can't have a second wife?" And he will be shocked by her response: "No, you can have a divorce but no second wife."

Why have I given so much attention to this serious matter of the home life and the responsibilities on the male? It is because I am influenced somewhat by a statement by qualified authorities in business who are conducting seminars throughout this country. As I said earlier, these authorities state that one of the main causes of failure for the small businessman is a bad home life. And most of that bad home life for us as African Americans is because we will not work hard to have honor at home.

Business is a need in human nature. Social establishment aspirations need to mate with business interests. If it doesn't, then you don't have much of a future for yourself in social establishment. We find this more when we go abroad. I was in mainland China and I was impressed with their belief that families were the best situations for the development of business. In Japan there is a model for that, where the family works in business together and establishes itself as a business group. It makes for better business in the nation when families become strong in business. Strong business families make strong economies.

When we look at the African-American condition, we find that we are very deficient in business sense and in business establishment. It is because we don't have business families. We have to insist that God wants us to have families with a business sense. That is the natural way that man has evolved. Man has evolved as a family with business development because of the needs of family pressing on him. He has to take care of his wife. He has to take care to have food, clothing and shelter for his family. There is no way to think of family, and divorce that interest from business. The two naturally go together. If you have a family, you have to have something to supply their needs. So the urge is to go out in the field and bring something back home. The problem for us is complicated because this world attracts us to influence us and get us to spend everything we made before we get back home.

As Muslims we can't allow that. Our men have to bring that money home. That is your religious duty and your need inside. Our life needs that just like it needs to drink, to eat, to exercise, etc. For a sense of social worth and social esteem in your family and in the society, for a sense of personal achievement in your family, you need business accomplishment. You won't have that sense of fulfillment unless you grow in business. We have to see business as an aspect of life, and that is the way it is for the economist and the business world. However, money should never be *the life*. Al-lslam is always *the life*.

A Muslim in Al-lslam is first to look for a wife in a believing

Muslim. That believer is expected to have respect for that life discipline of the Muslim family. Religions as Christianity, Judaism and our religion of "Islam" have a set and established form of behavior. That is a natural need and is most important. Even primitive man has a set behavior in his family. But when we come into the "enlightened" world of man and man leans on psychology and invents a new environment, original nature is suppressed. In many places man's constructions shut out the lights and the pure voices of nature. In a situation like that, we don't have much working to keep us in touch with the best of our human nature. For nature wants to achieve (evolve) and we have to have something as a set discipline to keep us going in the line of achievement for excellence of nature. If we don't have that, then once greed-motivated man closes us in with his commercial environment, we will become lost and cut off from the natural direction that Allah intends for human life in its excellence.

Our society has too many already living just for themselves, individually without family sense. Too many go out to earn money and spend wastefully on themselves, on a new car or a new wardrobe or on some entertainment. They tend to think that is all okay in the world of today. I have heard it said: "That is just normal now." Some of our women are saying: "I don't need him in order to survive. I'm educated and can make my own living. I can buy me some pleasure." This is the way much of the world has been going.

Natural Appreciation for Work and Family Dignity

What is also lost along with poor sense of family is the appreciation for work. The family is evolved naturally to appreciate work, and work is not supposed to be a bad word; it is supposed to be a good word. Work is not supposed to be a word that lets down our spirit. Work is supposed to lift our spirit. In natural life, play is work in the womb of social development. Play is work trying to be born. When the child becomes twenty-one, thirty-five or forty and is out there behaving like he did when he was a child, something is wrong. Now if he starts finding joy and production from play promoted skills, then he is well. He will be constructing something, cutting down a branch or digging a trench in the earth. He is accurate with his strokes. He is flexing his muscles and knows that he has strength and skills.

Man and woman were created to love work. Man in primitive society tends to sing as he works. There is the singer Harry Belafonte who sang about the banana boat, about cutting the bananas from the trees and loading them onto boats to take them to the market. I have also seen pictures of the documented life of primitive people who go out to fish. They will go out singing and trotting to a rhythm. Their life was not all about bumping ends or shaking to music. That was not what made them happy. Going to work made them happy. Their joy was going out to get fish to help the family, to feed some hungry mouths. We can see play in nature as work in the social environment womb. Mother nature's man loves to work and enjoys work, and if he doesn't enjoy work, something bad has happened to him.

Slavery has damaged the social spirit and the inherent aim in our nature. A lot of our negatively relating to work has to do with slavery. A lot of us are self destructive and want to destroy beautiful things. A lot of that bad spirit is the ghost of slavery: "Hell, this belongs to the boss, tear it up." This bad spirit can work sometimes in the other way, where we become overly attached. Both can be explained as affects of slavery: "Hell, the White man used to ride around in shiny buggies, and we had to clean for him and wipe off his horse. He would go out with his lady, and we couldn't do that. Let him look at me now. Here I am in this brand new Lincoln Mark X. I have a six-door Mercedes. Let me go out there and torture him." This person has nowhere to go, but he drives all around White people in his long Mercedes. But who is paying? He is paying money to "Whites" to get back at Whites.

Now if he would invest that kind of money in building up a strong family socially and financially, he would really become something and have social dignity. All of that buying for spite and show is going to come to a dead end. He didn't keep up his payments. How can he keep up payments with no more motivation than spite and show? When you have a grudge motivation, you are not going to be able to go too far. You have to work upon something natural and excellent in man. That is what the religion wants us to see. Allah intended that we be natural and that we pursue the natural aim of excellence in nature.

We try to respect those things that Allah has established for us to respect. Allah says to the child in Qur'an: "If your parent strives with you to take you away from the worship of Me, don't agree with the parent. However, keep good relationship with the parent in this life." Isn't that wonderful? See how important family is. Allah says in another place to us: "Family rights have priority with Allah." We are not to tell people to come in and give to the mosque before they take care of their family needs. We are to tell people to take care of their families. Relatives are to take care of their immediate relatives. That is first. What Imam in good conscience can be happy knowing that someone's rent is not paid but that person is giving money to the mosque? Their children need clothes and cannot go outside because they have no decent clothes to wear, but they are giving the mosques and Imams money? We first have to look to the family needs. If we all were to cooperate behind promoting attention to family needs, we will all benefit down the line of time. The result is going to be stronger families. Stronger families are going to be more productive, and more will be coming to the whole society. There will be more to spend with the businessman and more to give in charity. This will come as a result of us working to build strong families and seeing family success as a priority in the Muslim community life.

Peace be upon Muhammed, the Prophet, who established the Muslim family just over 1415 years ago. He said: "To marry is my tradition." He said: "Whoever is against marriage is not of us." That means that anyone who starts promoting celibacy in our community is to be cast out of our community and not to be regarded anymore as a Muslim. Prophet Muhammed also said: "To marry is half of faith." When we accept marriage, we accept social responsibility for a social institution. Marriage is supposed to be a social institution. Everybody should know now that if you are true to your family obligations, you are going to help the economy. You are going to be a great help to the moral life of that bigger family that you are in (the Nation), whether it is your ethnic group or neighborhood or city. You will be an establishment and a contribution to self and to society.

Imam W. Deen Mohammed,
Muslim American Spokesman for Human Salvation

The Muslim Owners Business Conference was held in Newark, N.J., May 27-28, 1995, hosted by (L-R) Imam Ali Muslim of Masjid Mohammed-Newark. Imam W. Deen Mohammed gave the public address on the Sunday of this weekend, which has been incorporated, in part, into Chapter 7 of this book. The Banquet on Saturday night had as its keynote speaker Bro. Aamir M. Muhammad, who spoke on how to "Make Your Business A Muslim."

2

The Common Person Dealing With Perception

Most poor people are suffering because they don't have jobs or they don't have adequate jobs. The jobs they have are not enough to take care of them. Others who are unemployed are not even bothered, and that is why they are not employed. Those who are bothered by not being employed, in time they are going to be employed. We have to try to reach those who are not bothered by their situation. I believe that many of us who are now very much alive and active and productive were at some time just like many out there who are not even bothered by their situation. We changed when something came to our awareness in the form of a message. Our whole mental disposition was changed. It gave us a new way of looking at things.

That kind of help does not come instantly. It comes over a period of time of being exposed to a particular sensitizer, which can be the Word of God or it may be something else. However, we have to be sensitized by something. The quickest answer I can give for making change, the change that we should be wanting in our lives, is to make a change in the way we look at things. The learned say that perception is all senses operating together. The common person thinks of perception perhaps as perceiving or seeing something with our eyes. That is perception, but the more complete meaning of perception and the richest meaning is that one which combines all senses working together. What we need is mental perception, perception to dawn in the mind and become clear for us in the mind. Many things affect perception, and perception affects all things for the individual.

VALUABLE ASSETS:
Faith and Trust

"Support from faith" is the answer. We have heard that "faith can move mountains." If you just had faith, you could accomplish and do so much of what you want to do. We need a conditioning to favor us having faith. Faith is not something we can come by easily. In fact, we say as Muslims and as people in religion: "No one can give another one faith..." Faith is always the Mercy of God. If we have faith, it is because of God's Mercy. Yet, there is plenty support for us having faith. When we use the term faith, also we are talking about trust. Faith and trust are almost the same, and in the language of the Qur'an faith and trust often carry the same meaning.

The life style and its burden on the individual person today and the demand on the individual's attention today make it very, very difficult for any individual to be in a situation to get help. This is a time that is described in scripture in these words: "No soul will be able to help another in any degree." No matter how much we try to help our friends or our own relatives, it looks like we are just wasting time - theirs and ours - when they are in that bad situation. But we shouldn't feel so let down when we call the community or the public to a solution and they don't respond. Most don't respond at home with each other. So why should we be disappointed if they don't respond when we call them? It is the times. Gradually, however, a change is coming about in the people's perception of Muslims. When that change grows and becomes clear, they are going to have the situation they need to act favorably. We are going to see a changed society, a changed public in this country. It is coming.

When we look at the world we may see it only in its physical picture. The world all outside of us and in us is a world of death and life. There is death and there is life, and the two are working together. As scripture (the Qur'an) tells us, the "dead is brought forth out of the living, and the living is brought out of the dead." That is enough support to generate faith. The world exists by a system operating upon this principle of death and life. Life, which is a mystery to me, comes out of death. Death, which is a mystery to me, comes out of life. Death supports life; that is enough to generate faith.

Closer to us, we have our own world of human beings and our families. In our families we see birth and in time death. We can observe the baby newly arrived today. It just arrived and we can see how its relationship is soon formed with the mother and how that relationship is so important for that baby to exist, live and grow to manhood or womanhood. Nobody can pay mother to be the mother God made her to be. She mothers her child from her (mother) nature. She will wake up in the middle of the night with fever herself and will be sick and weak. She hears crying and goes to attend to the baby. That alone is enough to generate in us faith in something outside of ourselves.

In our world situation, we should try anything that's rated high. We will see a creature who has lost faith in God. He has no time to talk about any "God." And some of us will see that person and will be so into religion, we may not even bother with him. But say you had a child and something separated you from that child. The child had no way of making a connection with you, but you had a way of making a connection with the child. Still you could not get that child to be aware of you as its parent. We know God can do anything. Even if that child heard your name, it may say, "I don't care anything about that person." But will that change your feelings for that child? No, even if the child said you did not exist or cursed the name. The child has been separated and has no direct way of communicating back. Also the child is not believing the communication that is coming from others. But that is your child you still love.

If you had the power, you would help that child and would be with that child. Whenever you saw that child doing something that merited a better condition in its life, whether the child knew you or not or perceived you correctly or not, you would give it credit for what it merited. If the child did kindness by another human being or by another child, you would give it credit for that. If the child woke up and brushed its teeth and kept itself clean, you would give it credit for that. You don't have to know God by His Name. You don't have to love God. Others will communicate it to you. But if you are good, you are going to get help from God just as though you know (accept) God. That is God; how can God be any other?

The human heart, our heart, is very special, especially when we understand or perceive the human heart as a free heart. The expression "free heart" means giving freely. To say, "He is a free hearted person," means that he is a giving or caring person. But I don't mean it in that sense. I mean free as a once slave is free or as a free thinker is free. I mean free as a liberated heart. We are given a free heart because we are individuals with freedom of thought. The Bible does not only mention thinking, it also mentions thinking in connection with the heart. "As a man thinketh in his heart..." (The Bible) This is a poetic picture. You are thinking in your mind but your heart is governing that activity, so you are thinking with your heart dictating. I find that most people think in their hearts.

The human being is a creature created by God to have free vision, liberated vision, liberated perception that goes outside of his small confines, like the sun appearing to rise up out of the earth to rise above everything below and around. The human heart with its sensitivities begins to reach not only that little small body it rose from but also the whole world. Now, if that heart loses the original nature given to it but still has that freedom, that is going to take the soul to hell. In time it is going to become a miserable heart. Freedom is too big a responsibility for any creature without support from Something bigger than creation itself. Call "It" what you want.

We know we don't see anything out there in the physical world that has the freedom we have. The sun is definitely important to the world for keeping us alive. But we also know the sun is not free. In the space that the sun is given by God, it is only following in obedience. Then look at man. Man can change. If the sun could stop its movement, it would be all over for the planets in the sun's system. We are free and have this advantage over everything created. The human being is not governed entirely by instinct. We have come out of that mold to change reality.

The animals are not "free." Although they are free to move, animals are locked in. Their behavior is limited to and already defined by instinct. They cannot go out of those limits unless we train them to do so. Animals have not evolved above the level of instinct-controlled creatures. Animals have never altered reality. They can go crazy but they leave reality the way it is. Human beings will go crazy in the house and then make the house crazy. The teacher will go crazy and make the students crazy. The preacher will go crazy and make the congregation crazy.

Governing Self

The heart is so powerful as an influence that it governs our mind, whether we know it or not. You don't devote your mind to something until your heart is drawn to it. This free and powerful heart of ours is too much for us to manage without the help of Something bigger. If the oppressed can accept that, then a new door has opened for them that was not there before. It is a door of hope. It is a door of new perception of my own reality and new opportunities. Persons need a perception of themselves and the perception of the reality for them in any given situation. It is the same whether you are alone with yourself or at home with your relatives or out on the job with somebody or in the public. Your reality should be the same for you whether it is in good circumstances or bad circumstances. Thinking now in that way should change the way you look at yourself and the external world. Whether from love molds, fear molds, greed molds, envy molds, hate molds, or others, the "free heart" is dictating to human minds.

We need something to motivate us in a positive and productive way. What will motivate that intolerable percentage of unemployed? We hear statistics about people who are on record as unemployed, but something should tell us those statistics are wrong if they are interpreted or read as the average one of us reads them. When you consider your typical neighborhood, you know there is more than fifty percent unemployed. The records we are hearing about of those who got laid off and are waiting to be rehired, those are the employers' figures. That does not tell you anything about the reality out there in the streets. The reality in these troubled inner cities is that unemployment runs as high as fifty percent. Most of these unemployed people are out of the reach of everyone; they were never on the records of being employed. Who is in touch with them, and who can say that they don't have jobs? You have to see them idle and the percentage who are idle to know that they are the unemployed. These are the chronic unemployed. It doesn't bother them that they are unemployed.

Many people come to employers to get jobs. Most of them will not be considered. When the applications are given out, many will not complete them and just get up and leave. These will not have a chance to even get an interview. Many of those who are approved for interviews will not show up. Most of those interviewed did not qualify. Their reading level was too low or their ability to perform the task was not there. So, they were not hired. Some will have criminal records and some will be on drugs. Who sees these victims among the unemployed?

Are we going to demand that our government spend our tax payers' money to create enough jobs to hire all of the unemployed? I agree that all of us should support eliminating unemployment if we are talking about eliminating that figure which is around four or five or six or seven percent unemployment. But we are talking also about the great majority of unemployed people who are not just African Americans, for there are Hispanics and others.

The "sex craze and violence" life style is killing the positive or productive initiative. But it is not enough just to tell you that. How do we make the people fit for employment? How do we make our youth, our young men, our males in this society fit for employment? We have to convert them to a new mind, a new way of thinking, so they will have a new perception and a new way of seeing themselves and the world and of the challenges out there. There is no other answer. But it'll be said: "We need a revolution!" What kind? A violent revolution? That is what we have out there in the streets every night and day, a violent revolution. Are we going to recruit those who are making our streets unsafe, who beat up each other and maim each other and kill each other over petty things?

If you can see the reality for you as a room or house or an entity with different departments, let us take a small apartment. It has a kitchen, a bathroom, a bedroom, and a living room. What happens in any of these rooms will affect the whole apartment. You can keep the living room beautiful, and people can come and visit you without ever seeing any other room. They will be complimenting you for keeping such a lovely apartment, and you will be taking all of it in. But if they look at you real close, they will see pain in your face. The other room is on your mind! It might be the bedroom or the bathroom or the kitchen. Any one of them messed up will also mess up your mind. You don't want to confess, but sometimes it is good to do just that. Say: "Wait a minute, you should see that pile of mess in the other room. I need help."

Each focus in the mind may represent a room. Each concentrated area in your mind represents a room. Race consciousness or race awareness will form a room. Unemployment and the situation for employment forms one room. Our own state and town and how they are performing also affects us. If any one of those concentrations of interest is out of order, it affects the whole mind. If we have the wrong perception of material life and opportunity, if it is terribly distorted, it is going to affect the whole state of our minds. If we have the wrong attitude or a distorted picture of what reality is for race relations, it is going to do the same. When people follow a discipline, an ideology, a philosophy, a message, a scripture, a teaching or whatever, that offers them a discipline for their total perception, a discipline that is in composition a total behavioral system - it decides how you will look at everything. When people have that, they are safe from those conditions most can't control.

Most of us don't want to really do justice by an ideology or a philosophy or a message or a religion. Although I hate to say religion, for the word religion is so loose and is open to so many interpretations. We need the right perception, and if there is a system offered for your total behavior, then you are safe.

The Bible said that the world was going to be destroyed and God saved it with Noah's Boat. And every living creature was put on Noah's Boat. That tale worried my mind for a long time. But now I understand that it is a beautiful allegory of a system for their salvation, a system for their behavior. All great religions offer a behavioral system. We need a behavioral system for ordering perceptions and attitudes in order to support us having faith in good behavior.

If we had a system of belief that was perceived correctly, patterned on God's universal value system, it should be able to support us and give us a situation for life and growth and prosperity. That is the idea and it will work. It is about motivation. We need something to motivate us. Some may say: "I am going to introduce my bad lost child to this person for help." You take him to the finest school, and make sacrifice and put another mortgage on the house. But that doesn't work. There is no answer or any guarantees that the help of this world is going to motivate these children or the adults. There are no guarantees, but there exist a strategy and a perception that work. We can keep ourselves to what we believe in; Muslims keep to the Qur'an and to the example of Muhammed The Prophet and keep to the excellence of our faith. This is the key for every human being. Every human being is created to want better. Don't be despondent and throw up your hands and give up because we can't get everybody to believe in the religion as we believe in it or think the way we think in the religion. Don't give up.

Work on doing two things. One is to educate ourselves in the Muslim community in the proper way; devote ourselves to that. Do that in our homes, in our schools, in our mosques. If you don't have such, then find a way to meet at least in your homes every week and educate your community in Islam, in Qur'an, in the Life of the Prophet. That is our first concentration. However, almost of equal importance is to help better the life in these streets of America. Those lost to the streets, have no interest, no faith and no desire to even accept good help, we cannot give up on them. Organizations like African American Men Against Narcotics (AA-MAN) in Dallas, Texas, and other urban areas are examples of what can be done to reach some of these "unreachable" people. When those who are lost see what AA-MAN is doing, some of these "unreachable" people are going to be inspired. It is happening; AA-MAN has had an effect.

Overthrowing the Burden of Myth

Work on improving the perception, not just the perception of one thing but the perception of the total reality. You won't see the results all at once, but it will be continuous and steady. When you present the Islamic perception of the total reality, all the natural laws and natural reality support that perception. You can call it scientific or whatever, but it will shatter the house of myth, troublesome fairy tales and none reality. We need to correctly educate the "perception" of the people. Whether you do it in the name of Islam or in the name of the Gospel of Jesus Christ, peace be upon the prophet, whether you do it in the name of one thing or the other, work on bringing the perception of man and his external world to agree with what is fact and reality in this real support system we call the world and space.

The American society is the most advanced society on earth in terms of science, industry and secular world advances. But when it comes to religion and culture, we Americans can be among the most primitive people walking this planet. That affects our cultural thinking. Myth burdened perception often does not prepare us for the challenge of reality. We can deal with small problems and can survive, but big problems eliminate us.

Most now who are advocating Afrocentricity are adding more confusion and more mind-locking myths. I love Africa, and I too advocate us becoming more aware of Africa. Since I began preaching I have been an advocate. Don't tell any more lies. Lies have our children shooting and killing each other and not valuing their life. Don't say they are unemployed and that's why they are in that state. We were out of jobs one hundred years ago, and we weren't killing each other in masses. We were freed from slavery and didn't have jobs, but we didn't want to kill off ourselves. We were only hoping just to have enough so the children could go to bed without hunger pains. We knew we were going to be hungry, but we didn't start killing each other.

The bigger part of the problem is blind behavior. The bigger part of it is the bad state within. The society is much responsible for it, because the media feeds lies about self and the external world. Any time an African-American youth is told the Black man is god, you are rigging him to destroy self sooner or later. He may seem to be doing well for a while, but in time he is going to become very destructive.

The answer is to go back to the original mother nature motivation. This original motivation is for improvement, excellence, betterment, growth, and growth toward more and more efficiency. The simple cell comes here and is not satisfied to be a simple cell. It splits and combines with other cells so as to become productive and more situated to do bigger things. All of the time it is growing, it is following a law of disciplined behavior. When we become conscious, something still tells us to want to do better. The new baby has a desire for decency, a desire for comfort. That comfort is to be clean. The baby is motivated just like that cell to become a more complex, a better performing, richer entity with bigger possibilities. The new baby is not satisfied to always sit or lie down. It wants to rise up. Eventually it wants to stand up on its own feet.

A child standing up for the first time is a feat of nature that makes you feel so happy. You share that child's victory. You see the fear on that child, but with the fear is the pride and faith in self. Fear is doing it the first time. The pride and the victory says, "Look! I did it!" And the baby joins us in walking upright. From a simple cell to a self-supporting individual there is a motivation toward betterment. Original mother nature motivation is help for better and greater performance. Life wants to do more and to do better. We need to call to excellence. Work for the society to be motivated by excellence.

Don't worry about telling them, "Hey, you are drinking liquor!" Do you think Prophet Muhammed, the prayers and the peace be on him, went out and the first thing he told his drinking people was, "Stop drinking"? No, our Prophet tolerated them drinking until he could tell them that God forbade them to drink. The first thing that he gave them was a real perception of themselves and the external world. That in itself created a situation for them to be motivated toward excellence. He reconnected them to their original excellence.

The Working Poor and Waste

Now, you are poor - we are poor. But at the same time the "poor in America" is both poor and well off. By global income tables or statistics very few of us are really poor. There are a very few of us who have nothing but poverty. We have televisions, beepers, $100 sneakers. That is what I call poor but big. One teenager will have a car and there will be two or three bicycles. But the family is poor and will get notices to move for not paying the rent. The phone will be off and sometimes the gas and lights too. But clothes are everywhere. I call them the affluent poor. That is what America has, an affluent poor.

Learn to respect money. In our religion everything deserves a respect. If you get $10 in your hands, then know that is $10. Look at what you need today and spend that $10 wisely. If you can manage today without touching that $10, then do not touch it. Keep that $10 for tomorrow, and try to continue day-by-day behaving like that, until you can save for tomorrow. I don't care how poor you are, you are supposed to save something for tomorrow. Cut down your bills. Move, if you have to, into two rooms if where you are now is too costly for you. Go where you can do better. Go down South, if necessary, where you can live cheaper. Before I let myself become a criminal or starve or see my family suffer, I would do exactly that. I would go to those extremes. But we don't have to go to those extremes. Start somewhere. Start by checking waste. Stop wasting. See the Qur'an on the fate of the wasters.

Sisters are a key factor for checking waste. Stop feeding your family everything that you can imagine. Stop catering wastefully to the family's eating habits. The people who are going to survive and will eventually end up being your landlords from among the poor or eventually will have that corner store in your neighborhood will be people with that determination and that discipline. They will sometime come from the extreme poor - Asians, Haitians, and others. They will struggle and make sacrifices. They will have two or three families sharing a three room apartment and some sleeping on floors, helping each other out, baby-sitting for each other. There will be one working one shift and one working another, so that someone will always be in the house. They will do that and will eventually become your landlord. Then you will ask the newspaper reporter or "7 On My Side" to come see the mistreatment: "We have been here all this time in this country and don't have anything! But look at these people how they are running their business in our neighborhood."

I am not saying all newcomers are the struggling poor. Some of them do get help. They may get help from their people back home in the country of their birth. They will come over here with money and will invest it here. Some of them are favored by the State Department, because our Government feels we owe them something for what they lost in their relationship with the United States. The government is paying a debt. I am not saying all of our complaints are not worth while. But many of our complaints are self degrading excuses for weakness and distrust in us and between us.

Why not try the philosophical approach. Just begin by saying we ought to discipline our spending habits, watch our money more, be willing to suffer a little to do better later. Search your faith to find that new perception of man and the external world that explains astounding progress for nations, past and present.

During the 1994 Annual Islamic Convention held in Washington, D.C., the Muslim Journal sponsored Exhibit covered the "Builder of the Nation of Islam" - the Hon. Elijah Muhammad.

3

The Promotion of Race and Business, How The Conflict is Resolved

We are thankful to Allah. We praise Him and we acknowledge that He Alone is God. There is no partner with Him. He manages the creation alone. He needs no help from any. He exists free of His creation depending on nothing from it. He is the Lord Most Merciful Who says that He created us expressly for His Mercy. We give praise to Him and we thank Him for the gift to the worlds of the one who is called "The Mercy to all the Worlds," Muhammed the Last Prophet, the Messenger of Allah, the prayers and the peace upon him, upon his descendants and upon his companions, all.

I would like to read some sayings of the Prophet as a great help to this presentation. When we know more about the Prophet himself, it is easier for us to grasp and appreciate what is being given to us of Al-lslam, what is given to us from the best sources for Muslims: the (Holy) Qur'an and the life of the Prophet, the prayers and the peace be upon him. This booklet on Prophet Muhammed's sayings has the spelling of his name as M-O-H-A-M-M-E-D. That was the popular spelling for a long time. The Prophet's name is spelled in different ways. The most unfamiliar way that I know of is the Turkish Muslims' spelling, "Mahmet." Yet, the name of our Prophet is pronounced the same regardless to how the spelling varies. It should be pronounced "MU-HUM-MED."

This book, "Sayings of the Prophet" by Saidah Chaudry, with illustrations by Pamela Howard, reads:

"It is better to sit alone than in the company with the bad. And it is better still to sit with the good than to sit alone. It is better to speak to a seeker of knowledge than to remain silent. But silence is better than idle words."

"Serve Allah as you would if you could see Him; although you do not see Him, He sees you."

"A Muslim who meets with others and shares their burdens is better than one who lives a life of seclusion and contemplation."

"Allah does not look at your appearance or your possessions, but He looks at your heart and your deeds."

"The best richness is the richness of the soul."

"Keep yourselves far from envy, because it eats up and takes away from good actions like fire eats up and burns wood."

"When three persons are together, two of them must not whisper to each other without letting the third hear, because it would hurt the third person."

"The person is not a perfect Muslim who eats till he is full and leaves his neighbors hungry around him."

"Conduct yourself in this world as if you are here to stay forever. Prepare for Eternity as if you are going to die tomorrow."

I have just collected a few sayings from this small example of the Sayings of the Last Prophet and Universal Messenger "Mohammed," the prayers and the peace be upon him. Those who have never heard sayings of the Prophet are getting acquainted with him now.

I hope in this reading it will enable us to come to the conclusion that we do have sure, positive, safe solutions for resolving conflicts of race and business. Racism is established in "message signaling concepts" that go into the social conscience to kill it. They are lethal concepts, deadly concepts, and Satan inspired those concepts. The world has been progressing toward a situation for man to have race consciousness and race esteem without having the burden of racism.

The Qur'an's enlightenment recognizes the natural inherent social value of race consciousness and racial esteem. I thank Allah that I have never been blown out into space from the realities of life. When you strive hard to please Allah in a world of confused religious language, that confusion makes it very difficult for you to see the clear guidance of Allah. It is easy to slip into endless confusion and never find ourselves. I have been able to keep the reality of what is my life. I am keeping my mind in the Qur'an and Muhammed's Sunnah. But there are the many in Qur'an and Sunnah and some are perhaps better authorities regarding it than I am. What distinguishes me in my own view is that I am also in my own reality. Therefore, in this regard I see myself with the few, not the many.

Creation - Supported Social Logic

Races and ethnic groups are distinguished by language and by color and by features. Of this, Allah the Dearest says: "These differences are signs." My color being "black" and another man's color being "white" and my nose and mouth being thick and another man's being thin: Of these distinctions Allah says they are signs. Also the difference in the languages we speak is also "a sign." In our Holy Book, the Qur'an, we are told: "Allah made us nations and tribes for us to acknowledge each other." Some translations read "...so that you may know each other." Continuing that Qur'anic message: "...And the most honorable of you are the most regardful." Some translate this as "the most God fearing." Also we are told that Allah gave us our design or our form "and made most excellent" our form. This design or descriptive form is given by God for all races.

Qur'anic enlightenment brings us to understand that every race and every person were created on the pattern of 'a full complete human.' That is to say that we all have this excellence in us as our potential and as a property of our creation. It is clearly given in the Qur'an that Allah made "noble every child of Adam." "Noble" means giving respect and being worthy of honor. "Noble" implies the best bred and the best blood. "Noble" also means that not only is that person worthy of honor to things deserving of that, but a person of nobility is the ideal person in the refined mind of enlightened societies. Some societies believe that certain races (colors) have no nobility and can never have nobility, that they are doomed to always be inferior to others. The ancient are the most known for that ignorance. Thanks to Allah, the Lord Creator and the One Lord, civilization, education and scientific information have worked along with good human sentiments to get rid of much of those ugly oppressive racist ideas.

Further quoting the Prophet, he says: "Allah is good and accepts only good." A better translation is: "Allah is good and does not accept other than good." I'm not giving anything that is unnecessary or of little worth. The word for "good" in Arabic also means goodness, goods and those things that qualify to be called useful by the best minded and most decent people. Another saying from the Prophet is: "The Muslim is the mirror for his brother." Let us see how powerful that saying is. If you want the best mirror, then get the information of what your appearance is and how you look from a good Muslim. Don't run to the dead object (glass reflector).

Two Attributes introduce each of the 113 Surahs (chapters) of the Qur'an and appears within the text of the 9th Chapter for a total of 114 Surahs. Every Surah of the Qur'an is accented by these two Attributes which say: "Allah is the Merciful Benefactor and the Merciful Redeemer" - Ar-Rahman Ar-Rahim. Both Attributes are having root in "Rahma" or Mercy. In order to construct the social benevolence of creation-supported social logic, the Qur'an offers us clear and positive guidance seen in the social role and benefit of *created* mercy.

The concept of man's beginning is what we want to look at now for a moment. According to most established religions, man had his beginning in Paradise. As pictured in religion, paradise is a condition of bliss, not bothered by anything. Our religion designates that condition as our beginning, that life (existence) formed first in Paradise. When something went wrong in our behavior, we were ordered to get down from that high state, to get down into the earth where we could have a place for all appetites. We are also told that in the earth is where we will reach the mark or miss it. Here on earth we will live, die, and be buried. **The Qur'anic quote is completed with Allah's Words: "...and from the earth you will be raised up again."**

The Qur'an clearly offers us the social benevolence of creation-supported social logic.

The Last Prophet said: "Who is not kind to our weak ones is not of us." This statement is a sign of Allah's Mercy to the worlds. An understanding of the expression "creation-supported social logic" may come with an observation of natural life. While observing animal behavior toward their young, human nature is touched by animal consideration for the weak. When we observe the "virgin" social life of animals on educational television, we may be drawn into their world to find ourselves admiring and applauding animal social behavior. I have watched the massive fierce tiger reach down and grab up its baby with frightening teeth without hurting it. The lion and the tiger reach down and grab up its baby with frightening teeth without hurting. How many of us present a more benevolent picture in our treatment of our young or weak ones? The lion and the tiger can take their big paws that can bring down other massive beats and with it pick up a pup or a kitten and hold it without causing it pain and scars. No kitten or pup runs to the welfare office or to the police department with a complaint of child abuse against its parents.

The point of view and the connecting sentiments being addressed are promoted by "Islamic teachings" and are preserved in the Qur'an and in the life example of Allah's Messenger Muhammed. To achieve the desired moral idea (moral regulation), creation-supported social logic is proposed as a holy medicine to say there is no "inherent sin." It serves world society to be aware of this cruel indictment of man's nature by organized (by defective) religion. The baby born to us comes here as it were from heaven. Our babies come into this world functionally and perceptually prepared to start a new chapter, a fresh record, a clean slate, another race (opportunity) for our smaller units of family and for "the family of man" another race for paradise.

Identifying somewhat with the critics who loathe organized religion for its excessive promotion of blind obedience to the discredit of the created worth and intelligence of the multitudes of innocent populations, I trust Allah Most Merciful to protect us from slipping and falling under the spell of worldly arts. Our being fond of a style of expression or an appealing effect we aim for is sometimes our own self-worked pitfall. I wish to never be noticed for having anything other than an "Islamic" concern for the premier cause of moral consistency on the part of religion. When one tries to gain a more mature appreciation for organized religion by faithfully examining it to see its moral contribution to moral consistency, to the peruser's regrets, a presence of poetic license is seen betraying, overruling, and selling out man's premier cause of moral consistency. More so than any other explanation, the belief in moral consistency is the influence behind my making my religious concerns public. Moreover, my enthusiasm for living, identifying, and projecting religious interest is the product of my conviction that Al-lslam ("Islam") is clearly the superior leader in this premier cause of man.

There is no excuse to be merciless to the weak; it is a breach of promise in the moral pledge of man. The natural mother accepts her baby and gives her baby the milk of virgin nature as created by Allah, the Lord Creator of everything. Cow's milk is nice; however, scientific reporting lists cow's milk under more fat, not suited as well to the infant taste, and of less value in the infant's system. Mother's human milk has agreeable fat and a kinder sugar. We are not to raise our children to have a taste for grease! The ease with which the substance goes down to digestion does not make it good. Mother's human milk is scientifically preferred mainly for its more compatible consistency on the human system. The mother is not growing her baby to become a bull to stroll around with its several hundreds of pounds in a greed fostering enclosure. Mothers of virgin human nature will not raise their children to live outdoors in the open ("free") air unprotected by human conscience and culturally sound and proven traditions.

Mother has the virgin mother nature to answer the needs of mother care for her child. Yet, in these times, many mothers are too burden by commercial life's circumstances to act on spiritual, moral and mental impulse. Whatever the case may be in "modern times" for the virtues of mother nature in our women, at her birth into this world, every mother had her creation-supported social benevolence. I have known mothers to be too sick themselves to be out of bed being up in the dead of night caring for their little sick ones. These mothers themselves would have cold and fever, but that did not show in their treatment of their babies. The beauty of it all does not bloom fully for us except in the creation scheme of Allah's mercy: "For that purpose (for His Mercy) He (Allah the Creator) created...." us. (Qur'an)

In some situations living for a cause is more of a sacrifice than dying for it. This acknowledged, death remains the ultimate sacrifice. Our mothers and also mothers "under" man in the scale of evolution are born having the creation-supported social benevolence to pay the ultimate price to save their children from trouble and death. It will help man to keep in mind the virtues of virgin life upon which the emergence of civilization was possible.

Most likely there would not have been the first image or shrine fashioned to the claim of man's divinity had society been encouraged to keep the whole picture. We should want to caution our societies against a temptation to drink from the strong wine of the seduced ego.

In this presentation, reference is made to our failure to awake to religion-promoted social concepts and social values. Such recognition brings with it a remarkable promotion for man's religious conscience. It brings man to a higher appreciation of religion and of divine revelation as complementing and affirming rather than negating or defaming creation and human nature. It is the ego of socially unevolved intellects that should be charged with the socially degenerative act of imaging "man" with a capacity to poison love and eclipse and demote the endearment to man of the concept "Creator," God.

The Creator's Divine Justice for Creation

The religion of the Qur'an informs that Allah (the only God) is the Creator of everything, the Giver of nature to everything, and that Allah has built and clocked into nature divinely given love and caring regard for "the little ones." Some judgment is brutal. But divine judgment is never blind and merciless. To be redeemed by Allah is not to be treated unjust. Merciful Allah's act of saving is never brutal. Man and society suffer the disregard for virgin nature and her prescription for controlling dependents. The abuse of the little ones by parents (mothers and fathers) in our private homes only became epidemic after an epidemic abuse of the dependent and weak populations by the industrial powers. We will go on hoping and praying for mercy to reach our big and strong ones for a more human vision of government and law to reign.

To embrace creation-supported social logic is to gain renewed determination for a sober humanizing behavior. Man (policy makers) cannot suffer forever his own ignorance and brutal policy. Many of the modern legislature have not been any better than the ancient powers who provided for the worship of the golden calf or for the destruction of the sacred temple.

As a symbol of oppressive rule, Pharaoh the oppressor had an amazing exaggeration of his own worth. When challenged and pressured to end the cruelty, Pharaoh's ego flared up to have him boast of himself being "god." Pharaoh's defiance and might are so power packed as a captivating piece of drama. At every chance to be spared, Pharaoh "hardened." Allah's Mercy was extended to this oppressive ruler over and over again. Pharaoh was never denied the opportunity for a change of behavior.

An oppressor's bullish insisting to have it his way against the way of Allah has never affected Allah's Mercy. Our commanders of the "turfs" obviously do not feel comfortable enough with their might to risk sharing authority. Their efforts are made mainly to hide and deny the merits of challengers.

Hence, Allah's mercy and grace are indicative and representative of Allah's Incomparable Self. Allah permits a bullish oppressor to take to the stage that will give the oppressor the world audience of the wise and the foolish. The foe is allowed freedom to delude himself and the world. Man is not prevented even from putting before the world a bid for the "throne of Allah." In the early life of man, the virgin nature was of the influence to bring sinners to repent and be redeemed. In our world today, the powerful influence of virgin nature is not enough for bringing man to repent sins against virgin nature.

The fate of moral life does not hinge on influences of wealth, education, or popularity in the world. For there are at all times persons on all levels of society who fight corruption and never succumb to it. Peace be on the Messengers: Prophet Abraham was known for his unblemished character amongst his people. The Prophet Moses earned his honorable deportment as a leader amongst the chiefs of Pharaoh. In the Qur'an, nothing less than the noblest esteem is paid to and attributed to both the prophet John and the prophet Christ Jesus. Like prophet Moses, our Prophet Muhammed earned his unequaled deportment amongst the sons of the famed tribe, the Quraish, of the Arabs. We have been in error believing Allah takes up filth to "wash away" man's oppressive sins. Decency is rewarded; sin is punished; repentance opens the door to mercy.

The world of greed and deceit fears the Qur'an and Allah's messenger Muhammed. Therefore, the biggest effort of the chief corrupters is their effort to take attention away from Islamic teaching and Muhammed's life. The advances against us by greed and deceit are mostly due to our blindly allowing our hurt and strained feelings to be used against us. The failure for the many is their allowing themselves to be manipulated morally into costly moral errors.

In the religion of the Muslims, the conduct of business and acquisition of wealth are also a devotion to the Merciful Allah Who is the Creator of everything. As people of faith, we need to stay aware of seemingly small but powerful truths. One such truth is to be aware of creation as a promoter of "good" consequences over "bad" consequences. Allah's Will is mercy; never is His Will to harm us. Another such truth is that "matter" is not evil. Allah deposited utility into everything created. The "natural" resources are given as utility to all people for all people. With Muslims, "spending" is to be seen as an exercise in the human purification process.

In the Qur'an, "creation" is put into context with the "message", and the message is, "We gave you your design." Again quoting from Qur'an, one Prophet was challenged by the disbelieving arrogant ruler, Pharaoh: "Who is this God you represent?" The Prophet responded with a powerful statement, saying: "God is the One Who gave everything its creation and thereafter gave guidance." He was telling that Ruler: "Although you claim to be God, God is the One Who gave everything its creation, you (Pharaoh) included."

The Prophet did not tell the Ruler "You too," for he was a diplomat, a skillful man, one who could go into the camp of the violent, mighty, unpredictable enemy and come out with his shirt still in tact. This Prophet did not address the powerful menacing Ruler directly. The Prophet said: "God is the One Who gave everything its creation and thereafter its guidance."

"Thereafter its guidance" says there is a necessary logic for connecting creation with guidance in a natural bond. The Prophet did not go by "four steps," for he was addressing an impatient and threatening Ruler. Also in the Qur'an, Allah Glorified says: "(Allah) created, then regulated justly; empowered, then gave guidance." It was more appropriate to address this Pharaoh's need in him to see all people with one and the same origin in matter.

The Conflict of Materialism and Profit Motive

The conflict for business and race is materialism: Allah intended that there be business, big business. Are you going to put some limit on how much money you want? Allah says to the boastful disbeliever, "Do you think We were at play when We did all of this (marvelous) creation?" Look at the sun, moon, stars, galaxies, the wonders of earth and all creation. Do you think Allah was playing games? Praise be to Allah. We have to purify the motive in business. In our religion matters are judged by intentions, and intentions are only accepted when they are innocent, not devilish.

The motive in the Western idea of business is to make profit. It is called the "profit motive." A few generations back theorists informed policy makers of the Western world of how the business future could be brightened by a bold and different treatment of the principle of "supply and demand." It was suggested that the answer was that they not be disciplined by the innocent law of demand and supply. The role psychology can have in the creation or in the forming of appetites was given as the lifeline of business. Any appetite could be cultured. So the idea was planted that anything could be popularized and given strong commercial appeal. Now sales promotions are determined more by the role of manipulative (behavioral) psychology than by the innocent rule of "supply and demand." That was a wicked turn for the worse in what was already a morally troubled business world.

Yet, policy makers also learned that there were still people who had an intelligent respect for consumers. There were those who could stay clearheaded through it all and never accept a business world using psychology to promote in consumers the appetites for any and all sorts of things. And so, the policy makers thought they would rest all burdens on the shoulders of the Prophet Christ Jesus (on him be peace): "All is made clean by his blood." They established what they thought would be accepted and rewarded in the judgment, only to be disappointed in hell. (Qur'an)

Now we have the expression "disposable income." What in the Name of God is that? I don't have any income to "dispose" of, to throw away. I know what disposable diapers mean. When the business world is talking about disposable income among themselves, they are talking about money for investment. But among us it is money for appetites of animal level existence: compulsive consumer spending. The evil is the "hidden motive" in business. But make business "halal" (permissible) by obeying the motive Allah intended. Don't think that the pig is the only thing not halal, not permissible. The worse pig is the pig in man's blind spirit. Allah wants us to know that we are not to eat pig, for "we are what we eat."

"Greed" in the Western idea of economics is a "greed" built into and promoted as the main economic resource. The main resource in the Western economy and business is "promoted greed." If you take out promoted greed, it falls. Western economy is morally doomed to fall until Western economic principles repent. This greed promotion factor requires that you be sold also what you don't need. And if you don't want it, if your intelligence tells you that you shouldn't have it, in the name of "business" have sales psychology take charge. On television everyone is buying the product. The persons in your dreams are buying it; why not you!? Then you start feeling like you have mistreated yourself and must treat yourself to that product. Greed is promoted by fear, love, pride, vanity, etc. This is the evil in the business life.

Profiteering means to go after something without any respect for moral obligation. The thing that heads the undermining of the social life is this profiteering. And now the big and the small in the media tell us that we as African Americans are not the only ones who have collapsed, destroyed, fragmented family sense. Other races are suffering the same evils. Maybe, it is "what goes around comes around." Allah puts it this way: "Your (policy makers') evil will hem you in"; you can send out your evil in one direction, but Allah has made the universe to eventually move it (your evil) in upon you. Your works will get out of your hands. That is the justice of Allah, the Merciful Creator and Lord.

Where do we find equality? Allah has created an equality for all. Allah said: "Certainly, he is successful who spends on his soul. And he is in loss who debased his own soul." He who invests that which is cheap, inferior, poisoned, polluted, corrupt is choking out the life of his own soul; he deforms his own soul. The other who feeds the excellence of his soul, spends on his own soul only what is halal and meets good standards is establishing himself, he is successful.

Allah has "approved commerce and trade" (Qur'an). Allah approved supplying legitimate needs and making income from business; profit is approved. We are not to sell someone something that is worthless or worth less than the price we ask. When we say we are going to make a profit, that is saying something in business language and something in simple language. A profit means getting more out of this than what was paid out. So, really we are not supposed to make profit; that is, the price is supposed to be no more than the legitimate value. But intelligent pricing should be the standard. Fools may be sold anything. The fool may not know the market price or the market value or all that pricing involves.

It is not legitimate business for Muslims to be unfair. The business people are the main force and focus for combating poverty. The business people came in the early life of the international Muslim community, and among them were persons of the character for dignifying and giving a good image to Muslim businessmen. And values and business disciplines are our greatest need now. We are not only needing business sense and business mindedness in the business people, but there is need also for business sense and business mindedness in the consumers. With our business excellence, we are a powerful tool in the construction of society.

We live in America and we have citizenship here. So do not separate yourself from your great dignity - past, present, and future. Also, I am a member of one billion Muslims. They will ask: "What is your name?" Tell them, "Muslim." Do not let this world intimidate you and make you feel small or awkward. If you want to know what geography I am in, it is the United States of America. If you want to know what center I attend or what ethnic group, I will have no problem saying African American. What religion? Al-Islam. What organization? We will not be identified under organizations, even if we belong to organizations.

Allah Most Merciful says: "Let there rise out of you a group that...will not fear the accusations of the accusers." Such group will not be intimidated by this world's invitation to vanity and ruin. When they ask you, "Are you a Muslim?" You are to say, "Yes." Don't hesitate! Your response should be "Yes, praise be to Allah. Yes, thank God for His Mercy." If they ask, "Who is your leader?" You should tell them, "Our leader is Muhammed the Messenger of God, the prayers and the peace be upon him."

If you are asked, "Where is your organization?" Answer them, "My family is my organization. But if you are asking what body I belong to, I belong to the international body of Muslims, *the Ummah*. We number one billion and more."

The largest population of Muslims is in Indonesia, a population brought to this religion by the influence of ethical, decent, socially advanced Muslim business people from the Arabs and others. Their Muslim business principles of excellence can be matched by us. We are not to think that this religion is an Arab religion with an "Arab" prophet. Hateful rivals want you to think that this is a religion for Arabs and that there are very few others believing in it. While it is the Arabs who are a small minority in the great population of one billion Muslims. It is even questionable whether Arabs are the leaders in the Muslim world. Allah chose the Prophet; Allah chose humanity, not a race.

I have become aware of an attempt on the part of the so-called major media - including the big business sponsored Black media - to impose their choices onto the African American ("Black") public. A role for us as Muslims on every level in the media is made all the more urgent by such hateful rivalry. I have also detected that profiteering media tends to present a picture of this religion and the following that came from the Hon. Elijah Muhammad as having appeal among convicts, ex convicts, drug addicts, the dregs of society. Let me quickly say that the people who supported Elijah Muhammad and his works were originally mostly from Christian God-fearing life. They were religious and God-conscious. The pioneer followers of the Hon. Elijah Muhammad over the many years were not from prisons and the crime world. We think of them as the "decent militant striving poor." They were moral people who did not like what had happened to subject the spirit and thinking of the "Black race" to "White authority" and wrong doings.

Being a Muslim, following the Qur'an and following the success pattern of Muhammed the Prophet, we end the trial and error syndrome. Muslims don't need a mediator or an arbitrator; that is done away with in Al-lslam. Our spirit is reconciled by 'Tauheed' - one creation and One God over that creation. So the question is asked: "What do I own?" Nothing. That is the attitude business people should have in obedience to *Allah, the True Owner.* (Qur'an) The philosophy and psychology for saving the person who is indulging in material interest is that of Tauheed. Keeping that philosophy will be a strong factor for saving human life and human senses. We are not mystics, but we accept that we own nothing. We are going to die and will leave all we have to other authorities. We do not know what will happen when we are gone. What we "own" might end up with someone we hate. That happens, even though we know legal documents such as wills and legal trusts are so important.

I was asked: "Is there no room in your religion for progress?" They wanted to know how can "Islam" stay relevant and keep up with the times if Muslims can't make any changes. I explained that we believe Allah sees ahead and knows what's ahead. There's no need for change. Do people think Allah can't prepare for anytime in the future and He is understood to be the All-Knowing? Allah knows the beginning and the ending of all things. We really do a discredit to our Concept of Allah (God) when we think to put the scripture down for editors' skills. No alterations are necessary. The unique feature of Al-Islam we want to be aware of is that with the Qur'an interjections or changes on the text are a thing strictly outlawed or forbidden. Our religion has done away with patching and stripping to make scripture serve man's weakness. Our religion deals with our historical developments, purpose and destiny. Our religion is the way of peace and unity for human existence. Our religion establishes how we should live to earn Allah's favors. Our religion is the religion of permanence and conscious moral, ethical, consistent all-around growth and progress. It is not a seasonal good.

The religion of Al-Islam deals with how man is to see himself. It deals with what man is and what his role should be in life, and on this earth and how to recognize "emphases and priorities." We do need Allah's Guidance in the whole of our life. We need Allah's Help for everything, and we understand and accept that Allah has greatly helped us already. This human creation is a powerful and productive gift from Allah, and we should make the best use of what He already has given us. The additional help we need beyond our means and limitations as human beings is the theme and main point of Allah's Help (Mercy) to man.

Common Sense

Those limitations depend upon the circumstances we are in. Circumstances will make us ill prepared or well prepared for the life that our Lord created for us and intended for us. In terrible circumstances Allah comes and gives us help that otherwise would be found in common sense, if those circumstances were not so confused and severe. That is to say, man at certain turns of events is helplessly lost from his common sense behavior and directional life. Hence, the Prophet dealt with a lot of issues that were people there who had done cruel and horrible things to Muhammed the Prophet, to his family, to his friends and to others of his followers. In this same town, upon achieving victory, the Prophet said: "All past offenses are forgiven. Let there be no more bloodletting."

Firmness, but also forgiveness, is the way of our Prophet. When we one-sidedly follow his character, we present a one-sided view of the Prophet and a one-sided view of the religion. I believe many of us do this in ignorance. Many of us have lived so long in a Crusade atmosphere where the "sword" and the "crescent" are in conflict. We have lived so long in that atmosphere that there has developed a kind of "cross and crescent" fixation and phobia.

I have been told that if one renounces his religion after saying he is a believer, that person is to be killed. Agreed, if it is referring to wartime and to turncoats. Civilized armies will court martial and kill turncoats in these modern times. If a soldier supports the other side, he risks being killed. Peace times are different. What about a situation where a person just came to a meeting, heard a sermon on the religion and got excited and said, "Yes, I believe, and I would like to be a Muslim today." And that person recites the shahadah or oath of faith without knowing the religion? Then tomorrow, he runs into a preacher of another religion who says to him, "Come to God; just say you believe." That person then says, "Yes, I believe." Now, you want to go out and kill him?

We need people with good clean minds and with love for humanity to see what Allah is saying in His Holy Book and then give us the right understanding. We need to be a bit cautious. Today many traditional authors think they are products of the Qur'an and products of the life of the Prophet. But many do not see a problem in their wounds and sensitivities. They are victims of the influences of centuries of foreign occupation. They are victims of foreigners who came to their lands and changed their institutions, changed also their way of looking at the Qur'an, and changed their way of looking at Muhammed the Prophet. Many are victims of centuries of occupation and are not qualified to tell us what Allah says.

When I hear something coming out that does not sound decent for human beings, I reject it. If I don't find any support for it in the Qur'an, I reject it. I have read in a Muslim publication that the Jews and the Christians are kafirs (infidels). We sent our complaints to the country of the organization. We are working hard here to bring sense and respect to our religion as it is viewed by Americans. We want to appeal to them and show them the true picture of our religion. We have worked and have accomplished a lot; we have people now looking at this religion and appreciating it. We are living in a new time with new circumstances.

Allah says in the Qur'an: "Say, we have no contention with you people of the Book. Our contention is with the idol worshippers." That is the teaching of the Qur'an and it is the way of the Prophet. When the government was established in Medina, the proclamation came that guaranteed the freedoms and the rights of the Jews to go on practicing their religion the way they had before. The same was granted to the Christians. Since then, civilized Muslim leaders and nations have carried on that excellent tradition. Christians live in Muslim lands. Jews live in Muslim lands. There are long periods of productive life during the history of Muslim Spain. There in Spain were Jews and Christians and Muslims all living together and working together and prospering together under Muslim rule.

America's vision of the destiny for this continent has been called divine destiny. They came here from Europe to realize the "manifest destiny." What inspired it, I believe, was passages of their Christian scripture and the wisdom of their great philosophers and teachers. And I also strongly suspect that they had studied the great life of prosperous Muslim Spain. It is a pity that their achievement was lost. It was lost because of the intolerance on the part of European nations that were jealous. They were jealous to the extent they fired up ignorant prejudices to fuel the Crusades. What I say is not any criticism of Christianity; they were not living their Christianity. They were still in the grip of their ancestral savagery and ignorance.

America has been influenced recently to see certain Muslim

leaders and Muslim figures as monsters of a strange psychological make-up. I don't see the Palestinian armed forces as monsters; I see them as victims of monsters. In my opinion, these monsters were human before driven mad by inhuman treatment. Human beings do not take on a monstrous image until forced by circumstances beyond their control.

Another Lesson Out of History: Southern Man vs. Northern Man

I have grown to look differently at the Southern White European American man of the once cruel South. I have grown to look at that time and the circumstances to see also Whites as victims. I have grown to lay blame on the Northern man and on the Southern man.

As long as we have the explosive sensitivities most of us have, we are not going to make it in the land of plenty. The reason why we have troubling and crippling sensitivities is that we ourselves are victims of our plight. We should know that many were rejects of Europe who were established over us in the South. Many were let out of prisons. If they would agree to work for landowners in the new world (America), they were freed.

Much of this abused lot of the Europeans settled in the South. The better educated and the more wealthy settled mostly in the New England area. America grew upon the New England area and the Southern states. The less victimized were settled in the New England region. The victims of Europe's more horrible abuses settled in the South. When we study their history we see many Whites were abused in the way they abused us, their African slaves. What they inflicted upon us was inflicted upon them in their European lands by those of their race who were their masters. Many of them were unprepared to treat themselves or others as human beings. They were often themselves criminals and social rejects in the eyes of other Whites.

There were great minds among the Southerners, but their majority were victims of a horrifying past. I look at them now and have a different attitude. It is amazing that this mistreated lot of

Whites did as well as they did. Both are survivors retaining our human nature's goodness. A deeply scarred people while yet festering should not have been given charge over our race. Babies born to slavery were put in the custody of these victims of Europe's cruelties. The South (its masses) was at the mercy of a monster formed by the hands of its history as victim.

Have you heard the story of the lost boy who was found in the woods? He lived and survived among animals. When they discovered him, he was behaving like an animal. He could not speak. It was the same for a child born into America's "peculiar" slavery. If you know the history of that "infamous" period, you will know it was forbidden for anyone to give a slave any literature. Slaves were not permitted to read a Bible. They were not permitted to have anything come to them of true history. Nothing was permitted to come to the slave except what would serve to keep the slave in subhuman animal condition.

Now knowing the circumstances which had a role in shaping the Southern man and knowing the circumstances which favored the Northern man, I have come to know how the Northern man played the "master" against the "slave" and the "slave" against the "master". The Northern man did that for his own selfish exploits. I know how the Northern man won the Civil War, occupied his Southern brothers' land and then used Blacks in reconstruction to rub salt into his brothers' wounds by putting the slave in a position of authority. The Northern man made the slave the soldier-in-command, and the White man of the South had to come to the freed slave to get permission for certain things.

When the North occupied the South, the Northerner put members of our race in positions of authority over Whites. We may be foolish enough to say, "That is what they deserved." But the White man of the North planned for the African American and for the "White" South. He knew it was not good for our future to put us over Southern "Whites" suffering the bitterness of defeat. The Southern White man was already saying, "Our own people have killed us, wounded us, dominated us, and occupied our land." The real reason for the Civil War was the freedom of the free enterprise system. The Northerners knew that putting "slave over master" would make any relationship for the freed slaves with former masters impossible. He knew they would never be able to live together in the South in peace. The Northern power holders had to eliminate all risks of "Blacks" and "Whites" ever uniting for a strong South.

The Northern scheme was to get us ex-slaves up North for the labor-hungering new plantation of Northern factories. Study the early history of America's factories; they presented bad health risks. Working conditions in many early factories gave us to similar humiliation, hardship and brutal existence. More lives sometimes were lost in the factory situation than were lost on the Southern plantations. But the slave only saw freedom. We have to grow with experience, and our senses have to become more sharpened with experience. It is not too late to look back at those circumstances and extract from them the lesson we need for today. The lesson is to never let the people who victimized you and dominated you and abused you decide your future while you take it easy. We are going to study our social situation. We will then be in a better situation to study our political past.

It doesn't make the scientist less human because he is not dealing with this matter from his emotions. He still goes home and grabs his tender little baby and kisses it. He feels good and holds his child while watching television. He is no less human because he has divorced his stormy feelings from the problem at hand, and African Americans have to be able to do that. African Americans must mature to the point of having sharpened sensitivities. We should be cautious when we go into new areas. Don't go into the White man's neighborhood with no caution. That is not your neighborhood. Also be cautious going into your own neighborhoods. Be cautious to respect the residents of those neighborhoods and not be hurt by them. There are dangers in the world. You can't expect one-hundred years of so-called freedom marked all over with decades of lynching and terrorist Ku Klux Klan and Jim Crow Laws to disappear for African Americans to drop our guard. Be humane in your neighborhoods at home with your own, and with outsiders of all nationalities be humane and constituted to serve your own protection should the need present itself.

Cooperate for the Good of All

Our religion requires of us that we do not engage or join any movement or activities to promote or support something that is wrong. If we join a movement or become organized for something, we must be right ourselves. Allah says: "Cooperate with each other in the effort for righteousness, purity, and reverence." Allah also says that we are not allowed to join secret meetings and secret organizations, unless it be "to promote fairness between men."

We can meet secretly if our intent is good and honorable, sincere and pure, and good for human beings at large. If we are meeting for the good of the human beings at large, for honorable and upright or righteous purpose, then we can meet in secret. There may be some of us who think we aren't supposed to do anything in secret. In this land of plenty you had better do a whole lot in secret. But you must be well-meaning and do not have any purpose that is not honorable, (as Allah says) nor do anything that you would be ashamed of if it were made known publicly. "Do not mix into the charity or into what you spend that which is corrupt." Do not spend the dope money for the progress of the society. Do not bring the money that you stole to the masjid. Don't give that which if it were to be made public, you would be ashamed to identify yourself in it.

Allah says, "And do good..." The Qur'an: "Do that which will be appreciated by a people who are refined and decent. Do good by others as Allah has been good by you. And do not spread corruption in the earth." In the view of such clear Qur'anic teaching we see we are obligated as Muslims to present ourselves always in our Muslim form and to strive for more and more excellence in terms of what is the overall excellence of a Muslim. Your virtues, your moral side, your intelligence, your rational side, your social life, your political aspirations, and whatever the particular interest or concern may be are always supposed to be honorable and upright. Moreover, we are to be respectful of the good in the society, whether it be to the credit of Muslims or not.

Muslims are to cooperate with those who share those honorable concerns. Cooperate with those who want this same excellence. We already have enough people against the decent public. Why invite more enemies? Our religion sensitizes us to grow in intelligence and to grow in virtues, to grow in appreciation for good common sense and decency. That is what we must be about. Our religion influences us to think before we leap, to plan before going out and getting ourselves involved in heavy activities. Do some planning. Putting it very simply, our religion teaches us to watch where we are going and to have light on the situation and circumstances at all times.

Of Prophet Muhammed, it is said that the revelation was given to him so that he may bring us out of the "oppressive darkness" into the light. The world in darkness oppresses us. When we cannot see what we are doing or cannot see the circumstances around us, we need light. Do not act impulsively. There are those who are talking about problems of race. They are saying, "Yes, racism is rising again." If racists want to occupy themselves with racism, let us be involved productively. While they are occupying themselves with such, I am going to see if I can do a little better in the competition to get wealth. If they want to tie their hands up with racism, let them. In America, no one has to be a racist.

I know what racism will do. It will tie up your brains so tight that you will not be able to see your way around in your own house. So why be frightened by the saying, "Racism is growing and rising again! You know they can turn the clock back?" I know they cannot. The clock is not in the hands of one race anymore. There are new circumstances influencing the time. This is a different world globally. America has to watch the global hour hands on the clock to know what time it is on the national time piece. There have to be circumstances within for managing those outside of us. And that is a major point for the "have nots" who are trying to make it in the land of plenty. We should take a look at our own condition out of a desire to be better situated internally and externally. Do more and complain less. We do deserve the same good treatment that is given to any others. But what are we doing ourselves about our own condition? Are we questioning it?

Are we trying to look for causes? That is the kind of sensitivity we need for making it in the land of plenty.

Perfecting Worship Perfects Discipline

Very few African-American Christians have studied the logic or the wisdom of Christianity. The great majority haven't studied the natural basis important to Christianity. Also, it is important to know how religion views history. Many religious leaders have not done any study, and for them Christianity is superficial and shallow. Those without insight and without a spirit to meet the challenge of heavier concerns will tend to do the lazy thing: spook you and not educate you. We have to be aware that we are a people "up from slavery" and more of us are to be equipped to make informed choices.

I can read something to you and pass on to you my emphasis and my reading. It may be okay if I am your friend, for my influences will most likely be good for you. But if I am not your friend, then it is not good. The note I wish to make is that a religion that gives you a man to worship is seriously problematic. It is heavy psychology to take a slave right out of slavery and have him worship an image-likeness of his former enslaver. I believe a lot of those Blacks must have been just "Toming" and lying, and in time it became acceptable and normal.

Allah's Law of Justice does not allow double standards. "What Allah has ordered for the Prophets or the Messengers, He has also ordered for the believers." There are no double standards. Allah didn't send the Prophets to live by one code of behavior and another for their publics. Allah didn't send Prophets and allow them to violate laws, do wrong, and obligate the people to do right. In the Word of Allah there is no moral conflict. There is moral consistency all the way.

Allah says He is going to put in the earth a khalifah. A khalifah is someone with responsibility for himself and for the good state of society, someone trusted with authority. Allah also says that He has given everyone something of His Inspiration or "something of His Spirit." We need to come into the spirit that Allah wants for us. To have something of Allah's Spirit or of His

Inspiration simply means that we have to be disposed internally to serve the Will and Plan of Allah. We are to serve with our whole heart and soul and spirit. We want to serve the Will and Plan of our Creator. That is what Allah created in a khalifah. He created one who was moved by spirit and nature to serve the Will and Plan of the Creator. If you have that, I can guarantee that you will be successful in the land of plenty.

Success in the land of plenty is more difficult than success elsewhere. The richer, the more abundant, the more affluent a society, the more complex, the more challenging it is to the morals of man. There is serious challenge on the spirit of man, the intelligence of man, and the nature of man. A highly industrialized commercial society challenges the mother nature and gives man his greatest battle. We cannot make it alone. We have to turn to the help that Allah gave us.

If Allah revealed His Words as guidance for us in times gone by, when the world was not so complex and not so perplexing, then we must understand that now in this critical time and in the time of plenty we have to rely even more strictly on the Guidance of Allah. Prophet Muhammed said: "The Muslim, whenever he endeavors to do anything, he seeks to perfect it." We should have that quote on the wall of every classroom in the Muslim schools. That will motivate our children to aim for excellence and perfection. That is what it takes to make it in the Land of plenty.

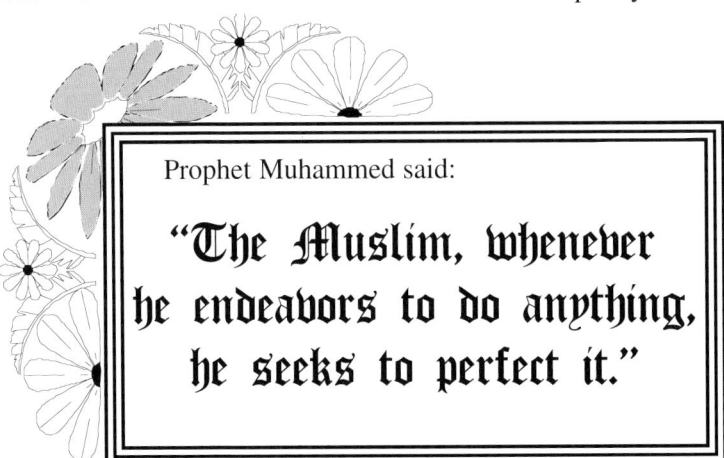

> Prophet Muhammed said:
>
> "The Muslim, whenever he endeavors to do anything, he seeks to perfect it."

Route To "The Destiny" Manifested: The 20-year celebration of this Muslim American Community in association with the leadership of Imam W. Deen Mohammed, held in Detroit, Labor Day weekend, Sept. 1-4, 1995, drew the largest Convention attendance ever.

6

Managing
The Spiritual and The Material

The management of material and spiritual concerns is only possible for us if we have something directing us as a Deciding Authority in our lives. There has to be an Authority in our life that decides authority for everything else and is greater than everything else. If you are not acknowledging an Authority in your life that you accept as having more authority than all else, then you are going to be a failure. Even the man or woman who look at their life in a very simple way and are unconscious of what should be the authority of God in their life, they too must be guided by an authority. Perhaps they are not thinking about religion or church or mosque or synagogue. They may only be thinking of how to be successful in their business life as employers or as career persons. However, if they don't have an Overriding Authority in their life, they are not going to be successful.

Understand this: Allah in our religion does not close the door of material growth on people because they don't acknowledge Him. Allah says in our Holy Book, the Qur'an, that the doors to those things are open to all. Non-believers can make money and Allah is not going to ask: "Did he take the shahadah? Is he a follower of Muhammed, My Last Prophet? If not, I'm not going to let him get rich!" It is not the way of Allah to close the way of material gain on non-believers. Allah says the doors to those things are open to all. But Allah also says: "But My special blessings are only for My devotees." Allah has blessings that are better, and you cannot get those without being devoted sincerely to Allah. In simple language this means you can have the material world, whether you respect Allah or not, but you will never be really happy or satisfied or pleased. If you want to be at peace, satisfied and feeling good about yourself, then you have to put your Creator before and above the world. You have to value the goal of satisfying your Creator more than you value your worldly ambitions.

No matter how saintly we become in this religion, we should never take on spiritualism in the extreme. We should never take on spiritualism to the degree that we begin to fear material involvement. Muslims are never to be called spiritualists. Work in the material field should never be thought of as a threat to the life we choose for ourselves. The answer given simply is to serve Allah, the God of both the spiritual and the material. Allah requires of us in our life as Muslims that we progress spiritually and in every other good way. No matter how good I am spiritually, no matter how good I am morally, no matter how good I am intellectually, if I have no material progress in my life, that is a sin on me. You may ask, "How is that, Brother Imam?" Allah says, "By what Allah has made available to you, seek the Destiny..., but don't forget your share of the world."

Seek the end, the paradise by utilizing what "Allah has made available." That means that in order to receive the promised reward of the "Hereafter" and to be in good shape with Allah, I have to use my moral nature, my moral force, my spiritual force, my intellect, my physical force, and everything in my possession. I should be marshalling everything in my resources to make progress towards the "Hereafter" (the Destiny). Therefore, a person in our religion who is working for the "Hereafter" will want to make a good showing in school. That person will want to make a good showing in education, in science, in business, in culture. That person will want to make a good showing in every good involvement, motivated by what Allah has told him: "With the means given you by Allah, seek the Destiny, and do not forget your share of the world." (Qur'an) Work to keep a good daily balanced account with Allah.

The prayers and the peace be upon him, our Prophet said: "Live today as though today is going to be the end of you." It means that we should not say, "Oh, we have tomorrow, we have next year. We will take care of it later." "Do not put off for tomorrow what you can do today"; that western expression says quite well what the Prophet said. Our Prophet also said: "Live as though you are never going to die." If I know I have a great many years in the future to go, I most likely will have some long distance plans. This is the way the Prophet has prepared us.

We also know that the Prophet has warned us against the pitfalls of material appetites and that we are to keep "the balance." We are not to let our material appetite hurt our intelligence or any other feature of our nature. Nor are we to let our spiritual life deny us the material world. We are not hermits. We do not withdraw from the world, no matter how holy we want to be. We never withdraw from the world and leave it to those who want dominance or corruption. Our religion is a complete life; therefore it is called "comprehensive," requiring that we devote attention to all important matters for the natural human being in the human society.

Fulfilling Lawful Obligations

The successful management of the spiritual and material is easy. Give devotion to Allah and regard Allah above everything else. Being obedient to Allah is what will save us from management failures. If in our hearts we love Allah and want to please Him above all else, we are saved from extremism whether it be materialism or spiritualism. Most important for Muslims is to see Allah as the God that asks of us obedience to Him. Allah asks that we fulfill all lawful obligations. We are to fulfill our obligations to our parents, to our families, to those who have assisted us, to those to whom we owe a debt, to the society we share life with. This awareness begins in what you owe yourself and goes out to your neighbor next door. Our religion is plain and complete in its instructions to us. Therefore, we should not be joining the blind herds for whom the traps of extremism (over reacting) are set.

There are some who have left the idea of their religion and have left the motivation that should be in all Muslims. That motivation is first of all to recognize the Overriding Authority in Muslim life. That Overriding Authority is Allah, the One and Only "Creator of everything." If we are having trouble with the management of basic concerns in Chicago, in Los Angeles, in New York City, or in Detroit, it is because we are not established in that Muslim life. To be established in the Muslim life we have to do more than just hear what it is to be a Muslim. We have to make a decision to be what we hear of the life from Qur'an and from our universal (the last) Prophet Muhammed. To be a Muslim is more than praying together and saying 'As-Salaam-Alaikum'. That is only a weak one-fifth of a Muslim life.

Being a Muslim is to obey Allah and obey the Messenger. Begin by choosing to favor reading our Holy Book. Be sincere and we will come to feel bad when we miss prayers. We will grow inside to feel hurt when we fail to obey religious orders. Whoever feels no weight of Muslim conscience on him is not successful as a Muslim. But if it bothers you that you missed your Maghrib (after sunset) or Fajr (before sunrise) prayers, then you have the religious conscience and spirit of the Muslim. If it bothers you that you are not eating halal meat, that you are eating meats of animals not slaughtered or prepared properly, then most likely you have the mind of a Muslim. If being in such bad situations bothers you, then you are in a good situation spiritually for the Muslim life. But if un-lslamic conditions on you do not bother you, we do not expect you to be successful as a Muslim.

Allah has asked that Muslims don't take intoxicants. And that means whether it is in the form of alcohol or drugs. We are never to drug our minds. If it takes our senses away or can affect us in that way, we are not to take it. It is the works of Satan, himself. It is a very serious matter. (Qur'an) Muslims are not to lie. If you call yourself a Muslim and you go on in the habit of lying and it does not bother you, you are not there yet. Perhaps everyone will lie occasionally, but some of us do have a conscience. We have to acknowledge Allah as the Uppermost Authority in our lives, as the Deciding Authority in our lives. We need an Authority to manage other authorities.

Do you know that the people who have the greatest difficulty in managing are the people who do not accept an Overriding Authority in their lives? One cannot succeed without rational guidance. We cannot be successful in our democracy without people who have intelligent disciplines and have respect for the power of reason, who think logically and plan on the basis of what is sound for the intelligence. We cannot be successful in competition with such people, trusting that the spirit is going to save us and deliver us while we do nothing but wait.

Unsuccessful Muslims are not in touch with the Guidance. Those who are in touch with the essentials to Muslim guidance are successful. There is no chance that rightly informed obedient Muslims will come to an end other than success. Allah says, "And the Believers must triumph." If we are sincere, faithful, and true to what Allah asks of us, we (the believers) must triumph. We have a history of those who were faithful to what Allah asked of them. We have a history of triumphant people (Muslims), people who are now being looked at again after centuries of darkness being over their true picture. This time it is the West that is beginning to take a sober intelligent look.

The Greatest Threat Is Spiritual, Not Material

The biggest challenge for the human being is to manage the whole life. The greatest threat is spiritual. What you cannot see is more difficult to handle. Spiritual influences are too powerful for us to manage without Allah. You have to have Allah. Allah has given us a body, and the influences of my own body will defeat me if I am not careful. We will see some people who have become so vain and so much in love with their own physical body, that the body sends them to the psychologist. The exaggerated love of the body sends them to the grave. People are dying with a disease called anorexia, where they are obsessed with the physical body looking good.

Our religion saves us by protecting for us that relationship upon which all other relationships depend. It is the relationship with Allah. All other relationships depend upon that relationship. If your relationship with Allah is right, then you are not going to have any trouble with other relationships that you can't manage. Our whole life experience tells us that. Allah said, "Do you think you will be admitted into Paradise just upon saying you believe? As others before you, you underwent hardships and were tested."

It is not right with Allah to take a certain group of people who say they love and believe in Him and spare them difficulties and leave other people to have the problems. If we accept the same burdens that other people have to accept and hold to Allah, we will deserve the Great Prize at the end of the road.

This world of profiteering people does not respect any definite life. I am not talking about Christians or the church, nor am I pointing at any particular thing. It is the world itself that is under the influence of greed, and it is not just material greed. The oppressors know that in order to get us under them, they have to have material power and a dominance. But they are not materialistic. You can go to their house and they will be eating small portions of food. They will spend money like it will not be around always. They will be in control of millions or billions of dollars. It is not that they are materialistic, but they eye material control over people, a control which some see as the throne of Allah (God).

The worst greed is not material greed. The worst greed is dominance. It is the greed for power over others. Those with that greed will sell everything - their mothers, their babies and everything - to keep themselves in a superior position over others. Greed for power, for authority and dominance is much more dangerous than the people who live for material things. The biggest materialist in the United States is the African American. Anyone who does not have enough money to pay the telephone bills for three consecutive months, but will go out and get a car costing $50,000, is materialistic. Anyone who complains about their race being behind and denied opportunities and puts thousands of dollars in a leather or fur coat is materialistic.

In contrast, the man who goes after material wealth and uses it to advance industry, security, and education is not necessarily a materialist. You should not be labelling people materialistic just because they have great wealth. I hope I can correct this now, for I have a plan to get us into big money! I hope to see this correction at least in my circle of associates. I don't want you looking at me and calling me materialistic. Allah says, "And My devoted servants shall inherit the earth." Don't you want that? I do! I want to inherit a piece of the earth with gold and diamonds and oil. We can manage it, if we always keep Allah first and highest over us.

My mother and father told me to be decent; not to lie, not to steal, not to go around with bad company. My mother, speaking for her husband and for herself, told me not to smoke and not to drink. And I feel so good to say today I have obeyed them. Allah does not charge us with what we do in ignorance without knowledge. Allah charges us only for what we do with knowledge. As long as the heart is sincere and truthful, Allah will stay with us and deliver us from a burden of confusion, ignorance and failure.

We have to manage our responsibilities in order to be successful. Allah has given us the Qur'an and the life of the Prophet. And the Prophet has demonstrated to us the responsibility that we all must accept. Whoever is qualified in our company, the charge is going to be made against them if things don't get done. If one person does not do what's needed, then the next one qualified should sense the burden of responsibility. Whoever is qualified should guard the interest.

We do our sunnah prayers. To some people it only means doing what the Prophet did. That is beautiful to me also, for I love doing what the Prophet did and feel obligated. However, the real beauty is the Prophet did them in addition to the congregational prayers. The real beauty is its protection against despotic rule. The Prophet demonstrated that every sane and abled individual Muslim must be responsible for leading him or herself. The same prayers that the Imam is taught, all of us are taught. If we have people come here for prayer, and the Imam cannot be found, any one male who knows the prayers can be the Imam. This is a religion that obligates its public to accept responsibility individually and to qualify themselves to the greatest degree. The responsibility is on us all. This is democracy in our religion of Al-Islam.

Islam: A Participatory Democracy

This is a democratic religion. It invites to the most advanced democratic idea. I can't think of one other that is more democratic in my view of what is democracy. Islam is to bring us to a participatory democracy where we are not satisfied only to have representatives. Islam is to serve us; for every man and woman no matter where they are in the scale of importance are to have access to all opportunities. Providing the persons qualify, they should not leave everything to their representatives. If they can qualify, they too should accept to be responsible and seek to answer needs. They should be represented in discussions of policy. Now we know we have a long way to go yet, but this is the direction. We are moving to where people in the general public will be responsible more and more for the life of this country, not only through their representatives, but also by their direct influence and contributions. Muslims, don't you know that is already granted in Al-Islam? We are trying to get there, but that responsibility is already ours in this religion.

In the time of Prophet Muhammed, he (the Prophet) made the people aware of their individual responsibility and if they saw something wrong, they knew they individually had the power to speak out and give guidance from the Qur'an and from the Prophet to correct the matter right on the spot. The Imam will be leading the prayer, and anyone in the group who knows that the Imam just made a mistake can call his attention to it by reciting correctly. That tells us and tells the Imam that he has made a mistake and he has to correct it. What other religion holds responsible the people in the congregation and authorizes the individuals of the congregation to correct the preacher should he be in error?

We have been taught that when Allah created everything, He created it perfectly to serve our best conditions and opportunities. We call it "Paradise." The real danger is misconceptions. We misconceive purposes. Therein lies the danger. There is a pig, an animal that Allah says we are not to eat. And, therefore we cannot raise the pig for somebody else to eat. But Allah created that animal. If you leave it out of you to its purpose, it is a good pig. It is only a bad pig when you start eating it or selling it to someone else for food consumption. Once in our community history we made the pig more important to our health than Allah. There were a lot of former Nation of Islam followers who had forgotten about Allah, but if the pig came up in conversation, they were prepared for it: "Man I will never touch any pork. How in the world can anyone eat pork? How in the world could the brother eat pork knowing all the trichinosis and germs in that naked big worm? I can do almost anything, man. But I don't think I could ever eat that filthy pig." That would be someone who could not say, "How in the world could anyone stop believing in Allah?"

The disciplines that we are given in Islam for our own life are the disciplines that we need for success. That is, no matter what the thing is we are discussing or thinking about, if we strive to please our Lord Creator, then we are assured success. I don't care what you want to go into, you are assured success. If you want to go into business, if you want to go into religious work or dawah (propagation work), if you want to be in education, if you want to be in medicine, you are assured success.

It is not always the rich person who is successful. Sometimes his wealth destroys his family. Sometimes his wealth destroys him. Sometimes his wealth lands him in jail. Sometimes his wealth gets him killed. The real success is "to be pleased." If I get all the money in the world and I am in hell mentally, I (in my soul) am not successful. There is no way to guarantee you are going to be rich. The guarantee is that you are going to be pleased. By that rule, there will always be more from the God-fearing group succeeding in business. Wealth with education does not always mean success. You can get all of the knowledge there is and still be needing a psychiatrist everyday.

Don't think any one thing is the answer other than the desire to please Allah. Everything else without obedience is not the answer. I remember a time in my life when I didn't have Prophet Muhammed. I didn't have the Qur'an. I didn't even have the right idea of Allah; I am speaking of the idea in the Nation of Islam. But I had faith in Allah. I had a belief that there is God. I knew I had to obey God, if I expected to be successful. I knew that He would judge me.

As it should be clear by now, the rule of disciplines is very important. There is a particular passage from the Qur'an that ties in business with the hope for success. It puts business into the focus with the hope for success. The passage says we are missing the real thing when we are going away from Allah to the dollar for success. This is the way I am commenting on it, because this is the way I am understanding it: "Oh you who believe! Shall I turn you on to a business deal that will save you from a punishing affliction? Believe in Allah and in His Messenger and strive in Allah's path with your possessions, your wealth, and with your own souls, your own selves. That is best for you, if you only knew." That is what God says in the Qur'an.

God used the term "tijaarah." Tijaarah means trade, commerce, business, enterprise. The term means something that invites and promises profit, something that offers material gain. Allah says: "Shall I turn you on to a business deal (Shall I turn you on to a business interest) that will save you?" He did not say 'that will make you rich', for many people are rich but they are lost. Then Allah tells us what to do: "Believe in Allah and in His Messenger." Allah didn't just say believe in Allah; "...believe in Allah and in His Messenger."

I wonder what would happen to date palms, if they were all left to most dollar chasers? It is hard for me to see people who are seeking immediate gratification planting date palms. Most of us don't want to do anything unless it pays us right away. I am traveling all over these United States to see something come to us now and to generations down the road.

When you have the mind to invest in something to benefit more than yourself, to benefit people after you are dead, then you also have the aspiration that will get you not only help from intelligent people, but help from God and His angels. This is because more than yourself, you are helping God's Cause. God does not only look out for us today, He looks out for our children to come in the future, generations down the road. Allah is not interested in just us; He is interested in all of the people now and to come. When you get that kind of interest, believe me, God is going to be with you and you will be successful. Of course, much of this is philosophical. But if you open your mind for the vision and open your heart for the sensitivities that Allah wants, you are going to be successful. It is guaranteed.

Remember God in the Business Day

In the beginning of the day, most people will say, "Oh God, help me today." And at the end of the day, most people will say "Oh God, lay me down to sleep in peace." But in the middle of our day when we are working and having coffee breaks and lunch, most people will not interrupt that time to remember God. If you want to hold up the throne, then interrupt that business stretch. Interrupt business and give God the respect and the attention that He asks we give.

We are talking about the keys for success in business. In order to be successful in business, I am saying that you have to first be successful as a believer in God. Be a successful Muslim. Look how successful the Muslim world was in the early days of the Islamic society under Prophet Muhammed and his great Companions. They became the greatest society on this earth, and this is in history. They led other societies back to civilization. The West will admit that it owes its regeneration to Islam, to Muhammed the Prophet and to the scientists who followed that revelation called Qur'an. Arnold Toynbee, perhaps the most popular and most respected historian for the West, pays great tribute to Islam in his report of history. What happened to this Islamic society that was so successful for centuries? They lost what we are trying to get right now. They got too busy with the world and lost Allah and consequently lost the world.

The proof exists, that by obeying the commands of Allah in the Qur'an and following His Prophet comes success. People came to Islam from backward life, from idolatry and no national unity. The Qur'an guided them to become the leaders of nations. When the Muslims stopped that obedience to Allah and His Messenger, they lost it.

There is a small surah (chapter) in the Qur'an that reads: "Concerning the time down through the ages, surely humanity is lost. Except for those who have faith, and their deeds are righteous. And they cooperate for the advancement of truth. And they cooperate for perseverance and patience" (Qur'an 103, Surah Al-Asr). There given are four conditions: They believe; they practice good deeds; they have as their aim truth; and they cooperate to encourage each other to persevere and keep patient. "Shall I point out to you a business deal, a commerce, that will save you from a punishing affliction....?" The first condition is to have faith in Allah and in His Messenger and to struggle in the path of God. You can see the resemblance for these two Qur'anic references.

There is no way to do mathematics half way. You have to do it all the way. It is either correct or incorrect. There is no way to run a business gambling. Some of us believe that we can go into business as gamblers, and our disciplines will be the disciplines of a gambler.

First, find a source to supply you and identify a market for your product or service. Know how much you can get out of that market or at least have a pretty accurate estimate. Play it safe, for business is not trusted to a gamble. Business is something that demands accuracy, and "truth" is another way of saying accuracy. If you are not working for accuracy, then forget about the material world. It is not for you. But if you appreciate the virtue of wanting to be accurate, you will be successful. Success for you will come not only in business but practically in everything. A good computer operator strives for accuracy. A good "anybody" strives for accuracy. A good march in the Army requires accuracy. Truth requires a desire for accuracy.

If accuracy is a must in the world for success, then truth is a must in your soul for success. Whatever makes for success in the world makes for success in the soul. Whatever makes for success in the human soul makes for success in the world. I heard an African American professor who did not know too much about true Islam once say, and I never will forget it: "Islam is not vain imagination or superstition. It is reality." Well, I can say today amen to what that professor told our class of University of Islam students. Islam is no superstition; it is not vain imagination. Islam is reality. We say God is Reality. We say Hell Fire is not a superstition, it is not a myth; it too is reality. (Qur'an)

God (Allah)

ISLAM'S CLIMATE FOR BUSINESS SUCCESS

A Great Signing - Imam W. Deen Mohammed, author of "Al-Islam: Unity and Leadership" autographs his new book at Pyramid Bookstore. Owner is Hodari A. Ali. This is one of the three stores owned by Ali located in Baltimore, MD.

7

Protecting the Business Future Upon Sound Motivations

Sisters, when you run your house, don't you know you are running a business? If it is an apartment, you are running a business. If you have children and a husband, you are running a business. If you have no one but yourself, you are running a business. A home is a business. The first health care center was home. The first lab or science department was home. Everything came out of the home. The first governmental order was home. The first school was home. The first bank was home. The first transportation center was home. If we get enough mothers running homes well, we do not have to worry about the state of society. The home gets the human being first.

The woman has to make herself a good business person for the future of her family. She should not go shopping with her appetites turned on and her brain turned off. She has so much money for a budget. She should shop with the knowledge of how much spending it can stand. She is to do justice by all of her concerns. She is not shopping just for the stomach or for clothes. She has water bills and food bills and the rent and school cost for her children. She has all kinds of needs to consider and costs to be aware of. I see another reason why Prophet Muhammed said, "Paradise lies at the foot of the mother." Our success at home means salvation for the streets and the whole of society. You kill your future when you go out and buy with no disciplines.

Best Policy: Patience, Sacrifice, Perseverance And Honesty

Patience points to sacrifice. "And cooperate for the establishment of patient perseverance" (Qur'an). This Qur'anic message suggests sacrifice. I have to sacrifice my appetite to protect something now for a more meaningful satisfaction later. We are sacrificing all the time. Sacrifice is a requirement in nature. We are no more savages throwing our children in the "fire" or sacrificing our children to please a god that we have imagined and sculptured. The real meaning of sacrifice is to deny what you want for now so that you may have a better situation later. Deny yourself until it is lawful, and accept that somethings are never lawful. Killing yourself is not the biggest sacrifice. To hang around hungry is a sacrifice. To stay around on earth and look at all of the good things in life and not take it, that is sacrifice. God says the sacrifice He accepts from us is our "taqwa". For anytime you obey Allah and deny appetites, you are making a sacrifice.

We must have honesty. A dishonest person can't be accurate. A dishonest person is not expected to be truthful. Faith and honesty are closely related. You can't be faithful unless you are an honest person. They used to have an old saying from the business people of the West that "honesty is the best policy." How many still remember that? I remember it from my boyhood. What happened to that? Honesty means faithfulness and makes for good and strict behavior. Patience tests your loyalty. Man must be loyal to his own image of himself.

Allah says in our Holy Book to Prophet Muhammed: "Say, 'I am a mortal just like you.'" Many people know that the one they claim is divine is a mortal. They know that he will die. They see him aging. But they will still say that he is "God." To eliminate any chance that we would fall into that kind of thinking, God says to Muhammed, "Say to them, 'I am a mortal just like you.'"

Prophet Muhammed was a man building friendships. Christians and Muslims need more desire to work for the common good. We can put down the swords of the Crusades and look at Muhammed with the eyes of decent people. When we see Muhammed, we see a man working on building alliances. We see a man committed to human decency, justice and peace. Even with the idolators who were his enemies, the Prophet made treaties. They often broke them, but still the Prophet made treaties with them. He was a rational man. Many of us would call our Imam an infidel or "kafir" if he would go to a known enemy of Islam to negotiate for better circumstances. But the Prophet did that!

We have to admit that our Prophet's situation was quite different from ours. In the history of the early community of Muslims, Muhammed for almost eleven years was not seen leading people in prayer, for prayer was not yet instituted. It was not until after about the eleventh year that he started instituting prayer for that first Ummah to pray in groups publicly. That time was a time that allowed for a total take over of one society by another. It was a God fearing society gaining control over an idolatrous society. In present-day society we are not in any situation to do that. We do not live in a "heathen society."

The Prophet pointed to the fact that it is not only concrete idol worship, but idols are formed of such as one's own pride. That is what the Satan was formed of - that pride that he could not give up; his big idea of himself. It is a condition on Muslims that we must believe in the Qur'an, and we must believe that there are other authentic scriptures or revelations that came from God. Although most scriptures have been changed by man's hands, we still have to accept those scriptures in their purity and originality.

We have plans for Muslims in America. The first step for success is to have a look into the future. Muslims, along with many religious people, are as travelers in the path. Whether you are riding a modern vehicle or riding a donkey, when you sat on that thing and start moving, you don't look in the present. Your eyes are not concentrated in the present. Your eyes are concentrated in the future. If you concentrate your eyes in the present while traveling, soon you are going to have a bad accident; at any rate, you will run off the road.

In the vision for the future is a determination to break from excessive dependency. When my father started, there were people pushing junk carts, working like a horse or a mule. A big donor had a junk cart as big as some of these pickup trucks. He would load it with rags, paper, cardboard, and scrap metal he found. You would see the secretary, Brother Ephraim Bahar, pulling it on the street bent over like a slave. He would have a heavy belt over his shoulder and attached to his junk wagon. When he came to "the Temple," he came in with a white shirt and tie, a nice suit with the pants pressed. Ephraim Bahar was a man.

Don't let anybody tell you there is no money in America for

you if you're "Black." There is plenty money in America. You have to have some industry in you to get it. Our religion makes it a religious duty to be gainfully and legally employed. You are not measuring up if you are not trying to get employed by legal means, halal means.

Wealth Must Circulate

In the Qur'an, Allah does not only point to the importance of business life, He also gives guidance for it: "Conduct the business interest in a way to prevent wealth from being monopolized. See that it circulates." This is a promotion strategy for the life of a society. The society can be oppressed by a strong business minority or a powerful business establishment. Islam must be against that. It might sound like we are socialists, but we are not. We are community people. Allah says in Qur'an that He does not overlook the worker's output whether it be a male or a female - both are to receive a just compensation (pay).

We understand that to mean women have the right to engage in business just like men. They also have equal rights to their production just like men. Whatever their effort and investment earned, they are entitled to it.

I recall reading the book by Ralph Ellison, The Invisible Man. The most interesting expression I found in that book for me said in effect: Somewhere along the road he found that he was "severed from his social responsibility." That made the whole book worth the money and the time I spent reading it. Allah wants Muslims to be financially and socially responsible.

I owe a lot to the Honorable Elijah Muhammad. My start was the Honorable Elijah Muhammad. He insisted upon us being responsible - responsible for ourselves and for everything in our charge. This was Islamic. He got this from the Qur'an and the life of our Prophet. We were taught by Elijah Muhammad to respect our families, our children, our women, our homes, and our property. We were also to be responsible to those who trusted us with something. The Honorable Elijah Muhammad said that if you worked for a boss, even if he were a White man, give him an honest day's work. Don't cheat him. He said if you borrow, pay your debts. Elijah Muhammad would write a whole column on that sometimes: "Muslims Pay Your Debt." Be responsible was what he insisted upon.

Muslim African Americans have an illuminating heritage as a people that goes all the way back to the continent of Africa. We want to talk about the roots of our life; we can't see our lifetime as limited to our life in America. We have to go back to the land of our ancestry, Africa. As Muslims in America we are now interested in establishing ourselves in America. By that I mean we want to leave institutions in this land in our neighborhoods that will stand for the generations to come. Those institutions will stand and will be supported by others from us who come behind us. The established institution of marriage in "Islam" begins with social and economic interest. Before you marry a woman, you have to have a dowry. The ring is a symbol and may be a dowry. Women in America expect that they will be given a nice ring. The more money he makes, the more the dowry. In the Muslim society, when poor, you may not have more than two chickens, but you are to bring her something.

Marriage is to embrace and grip a respect for money and the financial future of that relationship. A good woman does not want to form that relationship and you tell her nothing about how you are going to make a living. Some of us think that interferes with love. "Love" should not have to talk about money. My money I give is love and a necessity. If you are interested in a woman, then come with something. You don't talk about the money, you let the money talk for itself. After that you can then talk purely romance. Don't go to her with holes in your pants and you are not wearing designer jeans. That is not the way you go for a mate. Mister, you have to go to work and earn a steady income. This is practical, and if every woman were to tell you the truth, she would agree.

The dowry in an Islamic marriage is very important and should reflect the wealth or material standing of that person. The dowry in "Islam" is a security for the wife's future. It shows good faith and there is a dignity in doing that. With the dowry, you are saying: "I don't want my wife forced to go back and cry on daddy and momma or on her brothers and relatives in the event of my death or disability." You can become sick and cannot go to work, but you will know she has something for her support. If you suddenly die, she will have a mourning period of so many months and you don't want her during this period to be disturbed and have to go begging for her assistance. It may not be now that all of us can do this, but we all should be reaching for that self respect and social honor.

Healthy Families Mean Healthy Race

"What about the poor who cannot make any money?" We have to do something about that as a community and focus on the value of family and how wrecked families impact on the total society, weaken morals and hurt achievement. We have to devote our attention to it and do all we can in the interest of family. Let us work for the interest of the social life of man. Let us work for strong families and take care of those needs connected to family life, so that we will have healthy families and be a more honorable race of people.

Let us deal with the problem of unemployment in the interest of preserving the family and making better families in the future. That is what we should be looking at as Muslims, and I think that is what any civilized decent society would look at. We have to protect the family first. This is not coming only from our mouths. I am hearing it from Christians and from Jews. If you read some of the Jewish publications, you will see that they are having family problems too. All of us are having problems stabilizing the family in this modern, high tech grab-it-and-run society.

I want to address the rules of inheritance. When you read the Qur'an you find that there are obligations on parents, especially the male, to provide from his wealth for those who will outlive him. His wife gets a share, the sons a share, and the daughters a share. The shares are not the same. Sisters may flinch a little that sons get a larger share, but don't forget that dowry. If the husband is rich, the sister should have gotten a heavy dowry. The children don't get the dowry, that is only for the wife. In the Qur'anic regulation of inheritance, the wife will get a smaller share than her son when she inherits from her husband's wealth. The justice is seen in the way the economic system taxes males. The male inherits more than his sister also for the same reason. When the bread winner dies, the burdens fall naturally on the males of the family to provide for that family.

We have to be committed to struggle. The more you achieve, the more strength you have and the more willingness you have to have to sacrifice and overcome trouble. People are going to envy you. When you don't have anything, nobody bothers you. You are not important enough for the devil to talk directly to. The more you get, the more you will be envied and the more people will try to take what you have produced and carry it to their vaults. If they can't do that, then they will want to destroy what you have established. For this reason, Allah says to us, first of all, be reverent, be regardful; reverence the family ties. Be regardful of things that are very important for determining the outcome for you. Allah also says be faithful, be patient, and be persevering in patience. Some of us are patient but will not do anything while we are waiting. Be persistent and keep working on what you are committed to, until you realize what you are working and hoping for.

God says: "Struggle and form alliances." Muslims are supposed to be doing big things. And those big things must be supported by the first things, the most precious things. The most precious bond is your bond with Allah and with Prophet Muhammed. That is most important. But God also wants us to form alliances and bonds with others. We have the term called "breaking boundaries." We have to be boundary breakers. Isn't that what democracy is all about? It is about extending horizons and opening new ones. Be committed to break through boundaries and extend bonds, and work for better life and better opportunities.

Muslims Doing Business With Muslims

The Muslims of the United States, I don't see them firstly as members of any race or ethnic group. I see them as my brothers and sisters in this religion. I have positioned myself to explore the possibilities for me realizing a better life in America by joining hands with them. Many of us are coming into that same position to see that we are Muslims belonging to one international Muslim community. In this community we are one religious family, and this family has the best possibilities for realizing excellence. We are a big market of consumers but with an aim and a determination. Let's do business, Brothers!

We are going to test this American freedom, and we are going to test this great democracy. We are going to test its claim. We are going to compete for leadership in business in these United States of America. The law of this land allows for everything to be redone, even the Constitution itself. It says that if the people determine that the Constitution is not serving their noble aims any more, they are allowed by the provision in the Constitution to abolish it and write another one. Righteousness is the rule.

We are not going to impose Islamic life on anybody. We have a history to show that was not the way of our Prophet, and that was not the way of this Ummah's blessed followers. It is not the way of the Muslims. Spain was ruled by Muslims for about 700 years, and the Jews and others were allowed to keep their religion and progress worldly under Muslim rule. We have many other examples. We have India which itself was once under Muslim rule for 800 years. Islam's rule in India did not try to extirpate or do away with decent religions of India. The Hindu society is still there and giving the Muslims hell. Islam's excellent way of living and treating people eventually is going to reach more and more minds on this earth. People are going to welcome Muslims into their leadership of their society.

If there is a Muslim doing business here and a non-Muslim doing business there and you need something that the Muslim can give you, do you think you are supposed to go to the non-Muslim for it? That would be wrong. It is likewise for the Christians, but they are in a much better situation than we are. With the many Japanese and other migrants coming into American competition, things have changed. So we do need to buy American. I will put it this way: If we had the choice of buying from a newcomer from a thriving part of the world (like Japan or any other place) or from any born American, we should buy from the born American. There rarely will be the exception to justify that we do otherwise. If the American is selling me cheese that is molded and the newcomer has cheese that is not molded, then I might have a justification for buying from the newcomer. Allah does not obligate me to buy molded cheese from anybody. Nor do we just buy from a brother Muslim because he is a brother! That brother selling you inferior products, tell him: "Look my Muslim brother! You have to do better than this, if you want my patronage."

This will bring us up as a people with good social and good business sense. If we insist that we who are in business respect each other and respect all customers, that will add respect to our image in business. We want to favor our shopping with each other. Equally important, however, is that our business people be pressured to constantly strive for overall improvement in business. We are not to pass by the Muslim shop and give business to a non-Muslim shop. Your Muslim brother is a minority in this country and suffers a disadvantage because he is a minority. If he doesn't get the support of his own Muslim brother, then who is going to support him? Once he breaks into the market and is supported by the general market, we don't have to give him special treatment. But until that happens we are to treat that Muslim brother as a needy brother, and Muslims are to support their own needy brothers.

I am asking Muslims to support the Muslim in business and to support the immigrant Muslim in business. We are all the same (Muslims). If you do that, then I can negotiate for economic empowerment. The immigrant Muslims are in a better business situation than African Americans. They have more money to invest. They have a longer business history. While weighing and respecting concerns, I will negotiate for African American Muslims to get our fair share for what we may give others. We will give them respect and accept no less than the respect we give to be given to us. Let us not disobey our Prophet who taught us to be brothers loving each other.

Don't Lose Accomplishment To Seasons

Look to be like the tree. The tree works for its establishment. It has strong roots that penetrate deep into the ground. And philosophically speaking that tree has studied even the rock and takes on its strength. The Ebony tree is harder than some rock. There are trees that can break through limestone with their roots looking for water. We don't want to be weak and have our life taken away every time the four seasons go by. We want to have lasting establishment. We must be prepared to exert our mental powers, think hard and penetrate deep, powerful, solid and hard to unlock concepts. Strain your brain and penetrate those concepts or problems and send your curious mind down into those rocks so you can grow up tall and strong and last year after year.

The seasons will come and you will still be standing there; you won't have to start all over again. Most trees will keep their life even during the winter. But if they don't keep their life, at least they do not lose their accomplishments. Contrastingly, the grass loses everything that grew up; all that it achieved outside the earth dies during the winter season. The tree will look dead during the winter when the season is not good for it. What ever growth it achieved during the growing season, it keeps it until the season comes for growth again. Then it extends on its own accomplishments. The tree does not lose what it has achieved, and every year it gets bigger until it reaches its maturity.

The Muslim wants to have growth in his business and he does not want it lost every time a change comes in the seasons of business. You don't have to go down because it is winter for most. It can be winter for many and summer for you. Do you think these seasons affect those who control at least 80 percent of the whole world's wealth? Those who are thinking beyond the seasons may even gain during depression times. Allah says: "Man can have nothing but what he strives for and his striving will soon produce before his eyes" (Qur'an). He is to make a hard effort and not just with his hands, make a hard effort with his brain: Brainstorm.

Work hard to figure out a better life for yourself, to get the mistakes out of your business. Maybe you are in the wrong business and need to make a change. See if you are qualified for that business or if it will really reward you based upon what you can do and what your interests are. Tackle bigger problems, exert yourself more and be prepared for more difficulty. In time, you will have a much bigger establishment. Think progress and think and think over longer periods of time. A blade of grass is only thinking for one season; some trees are thinking all year round, for 200 years or more.

If the Hon. Elijah Muhammad said, "Let's have a bank," we tried to realize that. If he said he wanted a supermarket in Chicago, we tried to help him to realize that supermarket in Chicago. It wasn't because of any degrees he held in economics. It was because we believed in him. I am convinced that there are a lot of Muslims out there who believe in me; they trust me. And that is all we need to have real and big business; all we need is one person whom we can trust.

A Consumer In Your Own Market

I want an association of business owners. There are also others I want to be in association with who have great promise. They are people who don't have the capital and can't get loans. We want to organize. It is not going to be anything complicated, nothing tying us legally to each other. Even association is too strong a word, but for want of a better word I will use "association." We want an association of business owners and business-minded people who are already engaging in business. They are already supporting themselves from their business. Anyone who wants to join, all that person has to do is go into business. All wholesale investors must be able to show a positive identification, hold major credit cards and be able to show their tax return for the previous year. I have asked Allah to use me to protect this community. When the world knows you are willing to give your utmost, you will have open doors.

After the first group, go out and find others who may have bad circumstances but also have great promise. They will be those who come in under recommendation of someone in the first group. We have seen home shopping programs on television, which is a format we may follow. We will require that purchase money is first received before an item ordered is sent. We will find items that we think will be good for our community, and the community will help decide this. We will ask the people what they would like to see the community supply them with. We will not over burden ourselves and will start where we are strong. Remember that we are Muslims and consumers and somebody's market. We are weak financially because we are not our own market.

We know everybody uses toothbrushes and they don't last more than 90 days; this is a consumer item. But we don't want to be greedy on the expense of poor people. We don't want them to buy any more toothbrushes than they really need to buy. We don't want them to pay any more for anything than they are already paying. If we can't get an item to the consumer of the same quality and same price or lower, we don't want to deal in that item. We are looking at items that are easy to ship to a supplier on location. We don't need a lot of prayer rugs; a clean floor is better than a prayer rug on a dirty floor. We need garment factories. There will be no central office. None of us have any rights to any more profit than the other. The only thing that can justify me getting more than another person is if I had to spend more to get the product we wanted. It is then justified if the decision was made that we wanted to get that product through me. Then I have to get back that shipping cost on me. I should not be made to pay more than anybody else.

Each person who is representing a constituency will order for those he represents. There will be no legal ties; everyone will be responsible for his own business and taxes. The interaction will be to have a bigger volume buy. The bigger volume is what reduces the price on all of us. We will keep our prices at whatever the market is selling the item for; we are not after big profits.

In the long run our community will start showing material growth. We will begin to fund the building of schools and to better equip our schools. We will build our mosques ourselves and not rely on outside help. What we need most are strong schools and businesses. We don't want to have $2 million and $3 million tied up in expensive buildings. We also want to have our own insurance company. The power to insure is money you can have access to. This will include auto insurance and insurance for the home. We can give the same insurance benefits at half the price, because we don't want luxury cars and peacock offices.

Agree and follow me on a revolution. America wants to get close to China so that China will not be selling to other countries nuclear weapons and such technology. Look how the Chinese lived while they were growing. They lived in khaki pants fabric. They rode bicycles to work. We don't have to go to that extreme. But be prepared for some discipline and to do without a lot.

A Poor Community Rising To Wealth

If the poor of our community will listen, we will in time become rich as a community. A poor community that rises to a wealthy community will have the wealthy members. Help our poor brothers and sisters and see that they have a decent and comfortable life. We will have a big plan for employment. The priority is on making jobs available to more of our members, so that they can have decent and lawful income and won't have to go begging. This is for decent people. Those who like the criminal life, we don't have any obligation to help them. We have to stop trying to wait until all of our people get a good life. We will invite the poor to jobs and a way to get out of poverty, but we don't have to join them in their poverty. When it comes to the zakat or charity to the poor, know that the United States is already giving to the poor more than the 2.5 percent. We want to provide jobs to those who want to work and who want to pay zakat.

When we get enough resources and find people who can work commercial machines like those used in garment making, we can fix up someone's basement and secure it with 24-hour watchmen and start a business in a basement. If those home based factories are successful and the city sees the benefit of jobs coming to that city, the city officials will be helpful. We can have factories like they have in the Third World. When you have the cooperation of people, there is always a way to get around barriers. We can rely partly on a barter system. You give me your suit for my shoes. I will give you my computer for your car. This plan was introduced in Newark, N.J., on May 28, 1995, and it was accepted by nearly 100 percent in attendance. If Newark accepts it, I believe others all over the United States will accept it in the same spirit.

There are a number of difficulties that we have in America, and it is not just on African Americans. Most Americans live in this society from week-to-week and can never establish themselves financially. Keeping their monthly bills inside the amount of their salaries for the same amount of time is a struggle that continues. Most are never able to change that situation or to establish themselves financially. There is a need to gain the type of establishment where we are no longer living from pay check to pay check. And the religion of Al-lslam conditions us to be prepared for success and not failure.

Free Enterprise, An Islamic Concept

There is the need to invest. I don't know if as Muslims we are aware of "Islam" as a religion that encourages the believer to invest - invest your earnings and wealth so that it grows. Economics in Islam is a big and serious subject. There are some scholarly people in the West and in these United States who are doing papers on the economic idea in Islam - what it says about wealth and investing and the regulation of wealth. In their studies they are coming mainly from our Holy Book, The Qur'an.

Our Qur'an is the source for these Muslim scholars to get the picture and present it to the West. Islam can offer something to the West, rather than represent a threat to the West. And I am a firm believer in that. It will require that the West makes some serious changes, but the West could keep essentially its idea of free enterprise and not that of capitalism upon greed. Keep the ideas of the right to one's own earnings and the right to decide how one's own wealth will be used. That is the right of the individual citizen in Islam, so there is a closeness and a compatibility for the Islamic idea of economics and for what we call the American idea

- the free enterprise system.

Personally, I don't think we have too much in the history of Islam to show this compatibility with the West. It is because in the time of the Prophet, there were not the pressures on society to really get the fullness of the guidance in Qur'an for economic life. It is only now that pressures are on the world to come up with innovative concepts and principles for dealing with each other in order to be fair and just by each other with the wealth. Big government and high taxes have brought on the trend for American economists and policy makers and theorists to look desperately for new answers and new ideas.

We know of this economy and also of the global economy and of what the best minds are saying. Money has to be invested. It is no good for the economy or for the business life of the society or nation if money is going to lay up and not be put into service. This is Islam. Islam says that money should not be held somewhere rendering nothing to the society. Money should circulate and serve the needs of the people belonging to the society. Allah says in the Qur'an that the money should not be controlled by certain people so that it stays with them and not circulated where the society gets the benefit. This is good for any nation, and it is in accord with the thinking in American business circles.

When God says to us in the Qur'an to spend in the way of God, most of us tend to be so spiritual that we cannot see the real place for this idea. The real place for this idea is not up in the sky. The real place for it is down here where our business establishments and institutions exist. To "spend" in the way of God means to spend on ourselves and on others. He cautions us to not spend so much on ourselves that it appears that the hand is just bringing everything to the mouth. God cautions us also to not go to the other extreme and spend in a way that hardly anything is coming back to that person. God says this: "Do not spend so much that you make yourself a burden on society."

The money which is looked upon as an accumulation is that which is beyond one's reasonable needs. We know there are some who will say they need four Jaguars and six Mercedes. The society has to impose upon them heavy luxury tax. We have gotten this by way of legislature. Soon it is reflected in the Internal Revenue Service forms and regulations. This is what every African American needs to hear, whether they are Muslim or not; this is for the individual: If God wants us to invest, it also says God wants us to have something. How can I invest if I don't have anything? I will go so far as to say that voluntary poverty is a sin. The poverty that one suffers because they cannot help it is someone else's sin. But the poverty that one welcomes into their life is that person's sin. How is that person going to be of service financially to himself and to his family and friends, if that person is in need and doesn't care about his or her own future financial state?

God cautions us that if you want a strong family, don't trust the feeble-minded or the weak with your wealth. There are some of us who are simply ignorant, so look for those who show the most interest and the most ability to handle wealth and to protect that wealth, to invest that wealth and to grow wealth by handling it wisely. Trust those members of your family with your wealth and hold them responsible. Obligate them to care for the others. Don't trust those with weak minds and bad spending habits with your wealth. If you do, you won't have wealth in your family. Allah (God) wants us to be strong individually and to be strong as families. He wants us to have strong individual members in the society and to have strong families in the society.

Those who read the Qur'an will notice that God asks of us to spend more than He asks us to give in charity. If you count the number of times God says to spend and the number of times He says to give in charity, you will find that the number of times He says "spend" is many more. It is because the economy has to be strong. If we do not have people who are interested in creating wealth and investing it wisely, the economy will be weak and then the society. If the society is financially weak, opportunities are bad for individuals to have jobs and incomes. God also gives us instructions about our possessions. First, He wants us to have the right mind or the right way of looking at wealth. God wants us to be successful in the long run and in the immediate.

God, The Merciful Benefactor

Know from the very beginning that there is no chance for you to have anything except by the means that the Creator provided. A clothing business, a concrete factory with a contract with the city for building roads and sidewalks, regardless to what it is, there is no possibility without the means having been provided already. The Muslim is not to see himself as the benefactor; he should first see himself as the beneficiary. No matter if it be talents or skills or the resources of materials or the ideas pulled out of the sky after studying the needs in the environment and in the people's daily life for a product or service, the Muslim is to see himself as the beneficiary. The Muslim gives thanks to God first and then to other persons, things, situations, etc.

We should say "thank you" to the earth. By design Mother Earth gives us these things we need to work with. As a believer in God, we don't believe that Mother Earth designed her own nature and decided that she would have all of these treasures for human beings. We believe that a Creator did that and therefore we give the thanks to Allah first. Now if you understand the obligation to give credit to God, then the obligation to give credit to others starts from that point. We are also to be thankful to everybody and to everything that we get a benefit from. Our religion requires that after being thankful to God Who made it all possible, be thankful to parents, to adults who served as parents when we were dependent upon society and could not look out for our own life. Be thankful for whoever did the job of parenting for you. As you get bigger and see the earth as the producer of the things we need, then give thanks to God for the earth and have a respect for the earth. Care about the earth. If you will care about the $5 or the $500 or the $5000 you will have in your possession, the same kind of regard for all that supply you your needs will make you very successful in the world.

The Muslim is to teach his child to care about clothes, about the toys. Disrespect for anything is ultimately disrespect for yourself, and it means failure in life. If we could just instill due regard and due respect for property, we will see change in our lives for the better. We say God is the Absolute Owner.

What we have, technically speaking, is not ownership, but a trust. God is the only one Who can own; I am a trustee. So my ownership, though legal in society, by applying Qur'anic logic is only a trust. God made all of these things available and God decides who possesses these things. God decides whether the possessor will stay in possession of these things, and we also know that every possessor loses possession with death. Then its protection will depend upon the laws of society. There will also be circumstances in place which will determine whether the will and wishes of that possessor will be carried out. We know people who accumulate wealth and write wills and make trusts, and it does not always turn out that way. The nation can come up with new laws and legally kill what was the law before. Our Third World nations, we have seen, take over governments leaving citizens and others stripped of all of their rights.

Plan For The Future

God wants us to plan our future; He doesn't want us to have a situation where everything is by chance. We don't live by chance, we plan for our tomorrows. We are to plan for our children's tomorrows. God wants us to plan for the future of our society. If we can come up with enough resources and have success and become an influence or a factor affecting the future of our society, God obligates us to work for the good future of society. Society is first your family, then it is the people who belong to that community. Our society is our neighborhoods. If you hope for your children to inherit your house and live there also, you are obligated as a Muslim to care about the future of that neighborhood. You should be looking to see how you can use some of your money, some of your profits, some of your income to protect the life and future of your neighborhood.

If we have these sensitivities, we can rise. God wants for us the best. God says of us: "And the Believers must win." He did not say "maybe." He did not say "you should." God says to us in the Qur'an, our Holy Book: "The Believer must achieve success." This means there is no way for the Believer to be a failure, if he is truly a Believer. He or she is a full grown Believer only when he or she believes in all that God wants us to believe in. You can believe in making prayers, in fasting Ramadan, in God and His Angels, the Judgement Day, the Resurrection After Death - those are all wonderful; however, also plan for yourself and for your children who are coming behind you.

Don't see your children as other than yourself. Your children are from you. Know that your "life" is in those children. Their non-physical self is also much from you. We know associates they have will also contribute something to their personality and make up. We know teachers will be contributing something. But they are formed first in the care of the parents. The whole self is formed there. Certain interest and feelings for what is proper and improper, my taste for what is good and bad, my disciplines that keep me from losing myself in certain situations, I did not get that on my own. I got this mostly from my mother and father and sisters and brothers and associates. For me, it was mostly my mother who was with me practically all the time, while my father was on the road for many many years of my childhood. I thank God for my mother, and I will find myself cooking like I saw my mother doing in her kitchen.

Whatever we get from God, we should feel an obligation to God to manage it well and to respect it and to fulfill every obligation that God places on us. There is an obligation to myself personally, an obligation to my close relatives, to my aging parents. We should be on the side of those Americans who hate homes for the elderly. We know we have to have them because we can't do better. We should be with those Americans who want to change the system so that a poor son or daughter can care for their parents as they want to. We hope there will come a day when the government will have enough funds for our poor families to care for their aging members the way they want to care for them. If you don't have the facility in your home to keep your parents with you, then the government should help you get a big enough place and hire a person, hopefully a member of your family, to take care of the aged family members.

This is a futuristic social idea for many in America that I believe is coming one day. The interest and the motivation are in our scripture, the Qur'an. If I were a Christian, I could preach the same to that Christian audience and be coming from the text of their scripture. If I were a Jew, I could do the same before their audience.

Do not live only for today. Our Prophet said: "Live today as though you are going to live always." I should plan to have what I will need for tomorrow and for the years down the road. Plan for a long future; don't have a seven-day plan and then get a five-day notice at the end of the month. Have a 30-day plan and a 365-day plan and a 5-year, 10-year, 15-year and 20-year plan. Invision what you want for your children twenty years from today, and have that as a plan. Plan to save money for your children's education. Plan to work on a business idea with your family members. Plan a business establishment for your children to come into, even if you already have business establishment for yourself at this time. We want change. The nation cannot carry a growing citizenry of poor people with no checks on it.

The Dignity of The Individual and The Dignity of The Business

Let Muslims remember that Islam obligates us to accept that it is our responsibility to make some contribution to our community. Muslims should dislike their poverty and see it as an indignity, as something that takes away from their personal worth and dignity. Prophet Muhammed said the hand that is giving is above the hand that is receiving. The Prophet did not want us to be a community where the majority have our hands stretched out to receive.

Also, God wants us to feel uncomfortable with ourselves not producing but begging. This religion of Islam obligates the Muslim society to give money to people who are too proud to ask for it. It respects that pride in the person and obligates us by its laws to not just give to the person asking but to give also to the person in need but too dignified to ask for anything. That's an encouragement for us to have social dignity.

After our obedience to God, our focus becomes varied with many interests. As I have presented earlier, when it comes to Jumuah prayers on Fridays, God says that when Muslims have completed the prayer, then disperse into the avenues of business and profit; go back to your work. Friday, which is called Jumuah day, is the best day in the year. The Prophet taught us it was even better than the Eid-ul Adha and the Eid-ul Fitr, the two major holidays for Muslims each year.

On this special day for Muslims, God says: "Rush to come and participate in the Jumuah prayer, and when you have finished, then disperse..." God did not say, "When you finish maybe you would like to disperse...and go back to your business and make some more money." God said "disperse"; it is instructional.

If you are without the material success, you may have to beg. Go to the welfare office and you will find a lot of spiritual people coming there for help. There is no such thing as staying on this earth without any material life. God wants you to prove yourself in this world of challenges. Islam obligates all of us, even the poor ones, to grow up and to advance materially so that we will have dignity and a financial good future for the community.

Let us have a better and dignified relationship with the business establishments in our society, whether they are owned and run by Muslims or not. We need to know the value of those business establishments to the society. The habits of most African Americans make us weaker than other groups. We want respect for the relationship with the business establishment that supplies our needs. Look at other ethnicities and their relationship with their suppliers. People get into arguments with their supplier, but it is with the understanding that they will not abandon that supplier. For the most part, the African American's argument ends the relationship. Others will care about their "relationship" that they have built over the years with the supplier. They will argue but will not part company. Therefore, the supplier will listen to their argument and will try to please their demands. We all want to have that kind of relationship, one that we care about, and we don't want it just for today.

Predominantly in the African American community there is a record of treating his supplier or service businesses, his restaurants, etc., like it is a temporary love affair. He treats the restaurant in his neighborhood like he has no invested interest in seeing that restaurant succeed; he is unfaithful to his favorite restaurant and will change at a whim. It is like the poor husband with no family future who sees a pretty woman and is excited to get to know her. Then he sees another and is excited all over again to get to know her. You cannot have that kind of relationship with the businesses in your community or anywhere and be a success. Let us build a trust between our suppliers and us and between our customers and us. Let us have these bonds.

Tell that supplier: "You have a good store in this neighborhood; you have a good business in this neighborhood. We want to support you, and we want you to be fair by us. You are a good business person, and we want you to live here or to survive here and we want you to have a long future in our neighborhood." Talk to your suppliers. If one person cannot do that, then form a neighborhood committee to work to bring about strong bonds between their suppliers and their customers, and a big change for us will be seen.

Muhammed the Last Prophet was a businessman. His life was that of commerce and trade. He was employed by Lady Khadijah, may God be pleased with her, a wealthy lady. She saw such great future in him, that she turned her business over to him and he made it even more successful. She eventually proposed marriage to Muhammed, the Prophet and he accepted her proposal. So let us know the Islamic interest in its financial and business context and focus.

WHAT ABOUT THE MILLION MAN MARCH?

Imam W. Deen Mohammed gave this response to the following question at a Public Address in Decatur, Ill., on Sept. 10, 1995.

Q: What is your position on Minister Louis Farrakhan's Million Man March?

IWDM: My position, number one, is that this is not in the way or the practice of the Hon. Elijah Muhammad. He was very very strongly against marches on Washington or marches to the White House or marches on the government. He was strongly against it. He condemned the Civil Rights Movement very strongly for that. He said that instead of begging them and organizing to go demonstrate before them to beg for something, that we should organize to do something for ourselves.

Now, I think we need a million men marching on the blight and the neglect-property neglect, personal neglect, family neglect in our own African American communities. We need a million man march on our own neglect, that we are neglecting ourselves, neglecting our families and neglecting our neighborhoods. That we are not putting businesses in our own neighborhoods, just doing nothing and remaining idle as businessmen and business people and letting every other race put businesses there to serve and supply us with our needs. To march on that, I am ready. I will join him right now.

If he wants to have a million man march or a one thousand man march or a one hundred man march against that kind of thing in our neighborhoods, something to shock us into more responsibility for our own life and our own circumstances and our own future, if he wants a march like that, then I am ready to join his march.

But if he wants a march just to show President Bill Clinton that he can get one million young Blacks together, then I'm not going to join that. If he wants to demonstrate that we don't have jobs— which he hasn't made that clear—if he wants to demonstrate to the White House and to the country that, "I have a million men here who won't accept that we don't have employment and we demand one million jobs," I won't join him. Why? If we can get one million men to listen to us, then we can create a million jobs. All we need is a million men and we will create a million jobs.

If those million men, instead of marching on Washington, would just agree to buy from us, we will find talent enough in qualified businessmen —and if they support them and be hired by them, oh man, we will have a Black economy, an African American economy that is out of sight in a matter of days with a million men supporting it.

Thank you very much. Peace be on you; As-Salaam-Alaikum.

Imam W. Deen Mohammed assesses Million Man March, Sept. 29, 1995

When I made this statement in Decatur, no clear statement had been made by Minister Louis Farrakhan of the purpose of the march.

I whole heartedly support and urge our young African American men to accept responsibility for themselves, their wives, their children, their families and their communities throughout America.

This calls for more serious attention to the problems in the personal life, family life and neighborhood life. Our organizations should get involved. I am prepared to join Minister Farrakhan and the organizers of the March behind a serious effort that is neighborhood based.

I do not think a march of a million men is the better way to bring attention to the problem. The answer is not marching.

The cost of the march could be best spent on a business growth plan in the African American community for the purpose of hiring more of our African American males.

(This statement was sent to Minister Louis Farrakhan.)

A DIALOGUE AND DIALECTIC
By Abdul Mujid T. Mannan

"And the Firmament has He raised high and He has set up the Balance in order that ye may not transgress balance. So establish weight with justice and fall not short in the balance."
(The Holy Qur'an, Surah 55, Verses 7-9)

The Economic Balance

Utilizing the universal message of the Holy Qur'an and the Serah of Prophet Muhammed (PBUH), Imam W. Deen Mohammed transformed the battleground from one dominated by race politics and classism to one that challenges us to seek within the context of America's multicultural society the common mission of the Abrahamic faiths (Judaism, Christianity and Islam) in such ways that cooperative efforts can be made toward securing social justice, safer neighborhoods, and a climate for optimum human development.

It is within this context that Imam W. Deen Mohammed has penned this dynamic book, **Islam's Climate for Business Success**.

In this book, Imam W. Deen Mohammed underscores the Islamic perspective on business development, work and the socio-economic process.

Unlike capitalism, which seeks to maximize profits by simply preoccupying itself with the accumulation of capital at the expense of social justice and the fair distribution of wealth; and socialism, which relies on state-owned enterprises to accumulate, manage, and distribute wealth; Islam views business and work as a mechanism for attaining social justice, material freedom from slavery and poverty, and ultimately as a means of accessing a gate of paradise.

The Prophet Muhammed (PBUH) said, "The honest merchant is with the Prophets."

Within the context of the American experience, Imam W. Deen Mohammed identifies honest merchandising and honest trade as that which addresses the honest and lawful needs and legitimate necessities of people at a reasonable and honest price.

He condemns as evil the practice of profit engineering in American society, which creates artificial needs and appetites. The practice of selling the sizzle and not the steak creates enslavement to a chain of desire and dependency that malnourished the human spirit. Using the bodies of women to sell cars and cornflakes trivializes motherhood and degrades the human family.

Economics begins with the establishment of true values and ends with values that establish truth and social justice. Thus Imam Mohammed underscores that productivity is a process that begins in the cocoon of self investment in the family and the home economics of creating a balanced family budget, and balanced parental guidance.

The foregoing creates a climate for business success in society.

Imam Mohammed also condemns the enslaving notion that money is the root of all evil. In the 1970's, the flamboyant evangelist Reverend Ike said, "The lack of money is the root of evil."

Imam W. Deen Mohammed makes it clear that Allah, the Owner and Maker of all things material and non-material in the heavens and earth, intended that men engage in big business, but that men had to purify their motives.

The worse pig, he says, is not the pig forbidden to be eaten by Mosaic, Christian and Islamic law, but "the pig in man's blinded spirit." Islam provides the balance between both monkishness and materialism.

The Balance in Social Context of Forming Alliances for Socio-Economic Development

Muslims are a religious minority in America, comprising about 1 percent of the population. Islam, considered in some areas as the second largest religion in America after Christianity, is certainly the fastest growing religion in America. The influx of ethnic Muslims from Asia, Africa and the Middle East to America in late 1980's and the early 1990's, together with conversion of

American Blacks and Whites in record numbers, promises to make Islam a new dynamic force in the American marketplace.

Imam Mohammed, in this book, calls Muslims to understand that through a dialectic of dialogue among Muslims, Christians, Jews and other right-minded people, the adherents of Islam, Christianity, and Judaism can join forces to combat a Goliath-like materialism that threaten to destroy societal values. His call finds resonance in the tradition of both Jews and Christians.

Torah and rabbinic law underscores that wealth accumulation is for social distribution and for socioeconomic justice. See Leviticus 25:35; Deuteronomy 15:7-8, Deuteronomy 20:19-20. Hoarders are regarded in the Talmud in the same contemptuous light as those who lend money with interest; see Bava Batra Tractate 90B, Yad Mekhirah 14:5-6, Hoshen Mishpat 237:24.

The Torah forbids wronging people in business; see Leviticus 25:14. The Talmudic commentary of the sages states that "honesty in business is accounted to a man as though he had fulfilled the whole Torah." See Maimonides, the Commandments, p. 238, Mechlta 40:26.

Likewise, Christianity calls for accumulation and distribution of wealth and opportunity in accordance with the needs of the community, balancing the notion of achievement and contract with distributive justice. See Christianity and Economics, Schlossberg and Sider, 1991; see also Psalm 128:2, Thessalomans 3:8; 4:9-12; Ephesians 4:28; Acts 20:33-35.

Through cooperative alliance, on the common ground of one God, one creation, one humanity, Imam Mohammed calls Muslims, Christians and Jews to restrain the excesses of materialistic appetites in American society and resurrect the prophetic notion of distributive justice, equal opportunity and right conduct in business.

Conclusion

No doubt, the prophets of Allah, a brotherhood of perhaps thousands reflecting all human diversity, from Adam, Noah, Abraham, Moses, Jesus to Muhammed (PBUT) all came to establish two things on earth: obedience to the universal laws and decrees of the one true living God and "the Balance."

"The Balance" reflected in their messages and refracted in the unadulterated scriptures of Jews, Christians and Muslims alike (and others) is a balance that would right the scales of social justice and insure equitable distribution of wealth and equal opportunity/access to the marketplace of goods and education. This balance does not countenance nationalism (the putting of one tribe over others), cultural imperialism, materialism or the enthronement of any invidious distinction.

The earth is a miracle amongst billions of planets and stars in that it uniquely (as far as we know) has a climate best suitable to sustain human life.

W. Deen Mohammed, in using the dialectic miracle of the Qur'an, seeks to identify and inspire Islam's dynamism as a climate for business success within the context of the experiment and experience called America.

The American experiment and experience under the constitutional spirit allow in theory all men to enjoy life, liberty and the pursuit of happiness (wealth).

However, as an international civilization, so to speak, American civilization requires that its people, Muslims, Christians, Jews, Buddhists, Asians, Africans, Europeans, Pacific Islanders, Eskimos or Native people understand their uniqueness so that each can contribute to the common good.

Imam Mohammed's book distills the Islamic perspective and offers a balancing formula for establishing human and business success in America. It warrants careful reading and an open mind.

(Abdul Mujib T. Mannan, J.D. (Doctor of Law); New York University School of Law, 1984; M.A. (American History) Columbia University, 1981; B.A. (English Literature) Columbia University, 1973.)

ISLAM'S CLIMATE FOR BUSINESS SUCCESS

After his presentation at the 1995 Forbes Forum on Management in Naples, Fla., Imam W. Deen Mohammed (right) greets former U.S. Secretary of Defense, Casper Weinberger.

A Muslim Business Success Story! Supreme Fish Delight, best in quality, taste and service! Lawrence Shamsid-deen, President of Supreme Fish (& Chicken) Delight, has several other locations throughout Atlanta, GA.

In July of 1990, Imam W. Deen Mohammed personally presented a contribution of $85,000 to the Honorable Nelson Mandela. Three years later, July 6, 1993, Imam Mohammed (center) with his daughters - NGina and Laila - welcomed Mr. Mandela (left) again to the United States.

Exceptional - Nutritional - Affordable! That's Muhammad Ali Rotisserie Chicken, Inc., located in Baltimore, MD. Here Mrs. Muhammad Ali, known to most as Lonnie, serves the customers at its grand opening.

ISLAM'S CLIMATE FOR BUSINESS SUCCESS

(L) The Rev. Barbara Brown Zikmund, Pres. of the Hartford Seminary, presented Imam W. Deen Mohammed with the Cup of Compassion, Hartford, CT, December 9, 1994.

Persian art blends with the Islamic Minaret, an historic symbol for the Muslim call to unity in the gathering for prayer. It is the home of the New Regal Theatre located in Chicago, Illinois - the site of a major public address given by Imam W. Deen Mohammed on May 2, 1993, and the former structure used as an Islamic Cultural Center.

(L-R) Rev. Dr Lehman Bates, Executive Officer of the African Health Foundation, Dr. Hassan Abdallah Turabi, Secretary General of the Popular Arab and Islamic Conference, and Imam W. Deen Mohammed during the March 1994 trip to the Sudan with the African America Friendship Delegation. (Photo by Plemon T. El-Amin)

Sister Khadijah Nadirah, owner of D.K.W. Construction, Inc., a Muslim convert, must know the history of Lady Khadijah, the Prophet's wife! Sister Khadijah stands at one of her ongoing multi million dollar projects. She has already begun to provide her business skills to the Muslim community.

INDEX

A

Abuse
  natural order disregarded 46
Accuracy
  business disciplines 99, 103
Achievement
  material 65
African American Men Against Narcotics (AA-MAN)
  helping strategies 34
African Americans
  blind behavior 35
  business establishment relations 65, 122, 123
  doing for self priority 59
  family business sense 21
  illuminating heritage 106
  man's responsible role 19, 21
  problem of materialism 90
  sharpened sensitivities 70
Afrocentricity
  beware of confusion 35
Al-Islam
  comprehensive religion 17
  free enterprise 115
  obligation to contribute 121
  parents and children 75, 76
  participatory democracy 94
  peace 54
  permanence and progress 54
  premier cause 45
  promoting business 9
  solutions to racism 55, 72
  tolerance and revolution 76
Allah
  alliances encouraged 108
  angelic behavior 73
  assures believers success 66, 92
  believers accountable 61
  commerce approved 51
  created, regulated, empowered, guided 49
  Deciding Authority 88
  dominance seekers 13
  encourages investment 66, 116, 117
  excellence 10, 11
  faith is mercy 28
  family rights 24
  interest in all people 97
  Jumuah and business 16, 17
  man created excellent 42
  marriage responsibilities 19, 20
  material world 88
  merciful benefactor 7, 118
  mercy and justice 46, 47
  nature of mothers 29
  Overriding Authority 88, 90, 91
  parent-child relations 75, 76
  prepares for future 54
  progress 89
  racial distinctions 42
  signs 70
  spending and charity 117
  wealth circulation 105
America (U.S.A.)
  affluent society 70
  affluent poor 37
  diversity in business 17
  financial establishment 115
  history, north and south 79, 80, 81
  Muslims 78, 104
  peculiar character 69
  religious life permanence 58
  your share 15, 18
Animals
  merciful social life 43, 44

not free 30
Appetite
  manipulation 49, 50, 90
  patient sacrifice 102, 103
Attitude
  preparation for complex, serious 70
Authority
  Allah 88, 90, 91
  management 90

B

Bahar, Ephraim 104
Balance, the 90
Barter system
  business strategies 114, 115
Behavioral psychology
  business use 49, 50
Behavioral system
  protects man's life 33, 35
Believers
  guaranteed success 66, 119, 120
  obedience and success 92
Bible
  heart and thought 30
Blind behavior
  wrong perception 35
Brainstorm 111
Breaking boundaries 108
Business
  accuracy demanded 99
  business owners association 112
  excellence 11
  entrust to qualified 12, 17, 18
  financial dignity 121
  home first businesses 102
  long range planning 11, 12, 119, 121
  motive and interest 49
  Qur'anic guidance 88, 89
  success 14
  supporting schools, mosques 113
Business day
  interrupt and give respect 98
Business establishments
  seek better relationships 122, 123
Business people
  excellence 12, 13
  proper attitudes 52
  role models 51, 52, 98
  unfair 51
Business plan
  big volume buy 113
  include charity 15
  marketing strategies 113
  no expensive buildings 114

C

Children
  negative social influences 45, 75, 76
  parental influence 29, 75, 76
  plan future 119
  play prepares 22, 23
China
  discipline examples 114
  family and business 21
  trip 71
Christianity
  African-American history 84
  Crusades 77, 78
  established behavior 22
Christians
  family concerns 107, 121
  permanence with God 58
Civil War (U.S. history)
  lessons in history 80
Commerce, business deal 99
Common people
  industry and proper attitude 12
Common sense

Prophet Muhammed's example 55
Compulsive consumer spending 50
Constitution, U.S. 109
Consumers
  business strategies 50, 112, 113
Cooperation with decent 82, 83
Creation
  artificial 69
Creation-supported social logic
  humanizing behavior 46, 47
  rejects inherent sin 44
  social benefit 43, 45
Criminal 37, 61, 79, 103, 114
Crusades 77, 78

D

Democracy
  breaking boundaries 108
  participatory 94
Destiny, The
  business applications 9, 10, 11
  manifest destiny 78
  pursuit in life 13, 15, 73, 89
Discipline
  business strategies 96
  disciplined sensitivities 70, 72
Disposable income 50
Disrespect for self 118
Divine Justice 46
Divine revelation
  affirms human nature 46
Dominance
  corruption 90
  proper attitude 9, 13
  spiritual greed 93
Dowry
  marriage and finance 106
  rules of inheritance 107

E

Earth 15, 118

inherit gold, diamonds 93
Education
  improved 61
  working strategies 34
Ego, seduced 46
Eids 122
Elderly
  change care system 120
Ellison, Ralph 105
Employment
  big plan 114
  legal, lawful income 105, 114
  pay check to pay check 115
E Pluribus Unum 58
Equality
  reality based 19, 105
Excellence
  original motivation 36
  striving in business 10, 11
Extremes 72, 89

F

Faith
  principles of 59, 120
  valuable assets 27, 28
Family
  appreciate work 22
  business sense 21
  entrust wealth to able 117
  reverence ties 108
  rights, priority with Allah 24
  without sense 22
  work for strong 107
Farrakhan, Louis 124, 125
Feeble-minded
  do not give responsibility 18, 117
Free enterprise
  Islamic concept 115, 116
Freedom
  bigger support needed 30
Friday Prayer; see Jumuah Prayer

Future
  long range planning 11, 12

G

God; see Allah
Government, home 102
Greed
  arrogant dominance 13, 93
  economics 50
  motivated commercial environment 22
Governing self 30, 31

H

Hatred
  guidance strategy 16
Heaven
  conditions in this life 10
  signs 70
Hell
  conditions in this life 10, 13
Home
  budget, appetites 102
  first business 102
  salvation for streets 102
Home based factory
  business strategies 114
Home shopping
  business strategies 102, 113
Honesty 103
Human being
  biggest challenge spiritual 92
  functional 73
  help to govern heart 29, 30, 31
  home life first influence 102
  lessons of history 79, 80, 81
  liberated vision 30
Human creation 71
Human excellence
  primitive society 15
Human heart

  freedom of thought 30
  governs the mind 31
Human nature
  business a need 21
  excellence and growth 71
Husband
  look for wife 21
  wife and business 14

I

Idol worship 78, 104
Imams (Islamic leadership) 62, 63
India 109
Individual responsibility
  participatory democracy 94
Indonesia 52
Inherent sin
  concept rejected 44
Inheritance 18, 19, 107, 108, 119
Insurance company
  business strategies 114
Intoxicants 91
Investment
  Al-Islam's position 115
  benefit people 97
  courage and knowledge 65, 66
  obeying God 60
  strong family 23
Islam; see Al-Islam

J

Japan
  buy from 109
  family and business 21
Jews
  family concerns 107, 121
  Judaism established behavior 22
  permanence with God 58
  Spain, in 78, 109
Jibril, Angel 69
Jumuah Prayer (Friday Prayer)

138

importance 16, 60, 122

K
Kafir 78, 103
Khadijah, Lady 66, 123
Khalifah 84, 85

L
Land of plenty 69, 70, 71, 75, 85
Law of Justice
 no double standard 84
Lies
 destructive behavior 35
Life style
 new vision needed 28, 32
Love preached 16

M
Malcolm X 65
Man
 beginning in Paradise 43, 44
 change coming 28
 disregard for nature 46
 inheritance rules 18, 19
 loves work 22, 23
 marriage and finance 19, 20, 21
 responsibility 19
 role in life 54
 what strive for 111
Management 88, 90
Manifest destiny 78
Marriage
 respect economic interest 106
 role of man 19, 20
 social and economic benefits 24, 25
Masjid (mosque) role 63
Materialism 88, 90, 93
Media
 big business sponsored 53
Messengers (prophets)
 feared by greedy and deceitful 48
 models 47, 48
Million Man March 124, 125
Money
 honorable earnings 82, 114
 marriage, financial duties 106
 respect, not waste 37
 should circulate 105, 116
Moral consistency
 Al-Islam's teaching 44, 45
 beware of extremes 72, 73
 do not mix corrupt 82
Mother
 earth 118
 home management 102
 human milk 45
 natural role 29, 36, 45, 46
 Paradise lies at feet 102
Motivation
 the need 34
 spite 23, 24
 unemployed 31
Muhammad, Clara 64
 mother 94
Muhammad, Elijah
 business leadership 105, 106, 112
 early followers God-fearing 53
 father 70, 94
 idleness not accepted 64
 responsibility 106
Muhammed, Prophet (PBUH)
 benefits for humanity 73, 83
 brothers loving one another 110
 built alliances 103
 business example 66, 123
 called to excellence 36
 common sense man 54, 55
 demonstrated responsibility 94

139

discouraged begging 121
firmness and forgiveness 76, 77
importance of Jumuah 16
live as forever, as end 89, 90
marriage and family 24
mortal 103
persecuted 76
sayings of 12, 40, 41, 42, 43, 49, 63, 73, 85, 89, 102, 121

Muslim(s)
cooperation 82, 83
doing business with self 108, 109, 110
educate perception 31, 32, 33
financial, social responsibility 105
fulfill obligations 90
history 92
leader of 52
life in U.S.A. 104, 108
manage self 70
no moral conflict 14
not demogagues 74
not intimidated 52
not spiritualists 89
permanence with Allah 58
renounce, turncoat 77
thanks to God 118
view of dominance 13, 90
welcomed in leadership 109

Muslim African Americans
building institutions 106
recovered, renewed and productive 60
responsibility to invest 65

Muslim life
conscience 90, 91

Myth 35

N

Noah's Boat (ark)
protecting behavior system 33
North, the (U.S.) 80, 81

O

Obedience
faith and success 98
saves from failure 94

Oppressors
commanders of turfs 47
divine justice 46, 48
Pharaoh 47
seek dominance 93

Organized religions 44

Ownership
proper attitude 53, 119

P

Palestinians 79
Parents 29, 75, 76, 118
Participatory democracy 94
Passions
self, business management 14
Patience 102
Perception
behavioral system 31, 33
factors for change 27
Personal management 14
Permanence
establishment with God 58
Pig 95, 96
Polygamy
financial duties 20
Poor, the
affluent poor 37
business strategies 114
struggling poor 38
unreachable people 34
working poor 37, 62
Poverty
Muslims dislike 121

voluntary condition is sin 117
Prayer (Salat) 120
   lessons in democracy 94
Preparation
   meeting challenges 69, 70
Profit
   Allah's guidance 51
Profit motive
   Western economy 49
Profiteering 51, 53, 93
Promoted greed 50, 93
Psychology
   manipulative use 49
Public, the
   responsibility obligation 94, 95
Pygmy (people)
   natural human excellence 15

Q

Qur'an, Holy
   business excellence rewarded 11
   changes forbidden 54
   concept of The Destiny 9
   death supports life 28
   good business sense 17
   guidance on inheritance 18, 19
   guide for economics 115, 116
   leaving a will 18
   parents 24
   social value of race 41, 42

R

Race consciousness
   healthy 107
   Qur'anic guidance 33, 41, 42
Racial esteem
   Qur'anic guidance 42
Racism
   manner of establishment 16, 42
   proper sensitivity 83
Regardfulness

business success factors 14
   proper respect 108, 118
Religion
   affirms creation 43
   Al-Islam comprehensive 17, 22, 58, 90
   Christianity 22, 58, 77, 78, 84, 107, 121
   Jews, Judaism 22, 58, 107, 121
   protecting behavioral system 33
Responsibility
   Prophet Muhammed's example 94
   social and economic 106
   Qur'an and business 19
Resurrection 61
Revolution 32, 76, 114

S

Sacrifice 102, 103
Salat (Prayer) 59, 91
   against despotic rule 94
   lessons in democracy 94
Sales
   commercial appeal 49
Satan
   racist concepts inspired 41
Self pride 104
Seasonal business
   proper attitude 12, 111
Secrecy
   cooperation and guidance 82, 83
Sharpened sensitivities 70, 72
Slavery
   freedom from 35
   lessons in history 79, 80, 81
   natural spirit damaged 23
   worship image-likeness enslaver 84
Society
   kind to weak 43, 45
   suffers disregard for nature 46

Soul
  spends on it 51
  truth, accuracy and success 99
South, the (U.S.) 79, 80, 81
Spain
  history of Muslim rule 108
  Islam and tolerance 78
Spending
  investment encouraged 116, 117
  wasteful 22
Struggle 108
Success
  believer must achieve 120
  business 14
  devotion to Allah 120
  divine guidance needed 92
  found in obedience 98
  help from God 97
Sunnah prayers
  protection against oppression 94
Supply and demand 49, 113

T

Tolerance
  Prophet Muhammed's example 76, 77
Toynbee, Arnold 98
Tree
  don't lose accomplishment 111
Truth
  necessity for success 99

U

Ummah (Muslim community) 52, 109
Unemployment
  problems and solutions 31, 32, 107
United Negro College Fund 60

V

Victims
  lessons in history 79, 80, 81
Virgin nature
  created by Allah 44, 45, 46

W

War 69
Waste
  must be checked 37
Wealth
  acquisition and use 119
  circulation required 105, 116
  competition 83
  not socialists 105
  used to advance 93
Western world (The West)
  Islamic idea of economics 115, 116
  profit motive 50
Wife
  dowry, future 106
  husband and business 14
  rules of inheritance 18, 19, 107, 108
Will (estate)
  inheritance and responsibility 18, 19, 119
Woman (women)
  check wasteful spending 37
  have the first business 102
  inheritance 18, 19, 107, 108
  just compensation 105
  loves work 23
  marriage and finance 19, 20
  mothering nature 29, 36, 45, 46
  rights to wealth 19, 20
Work
  appreciate natural development 22
World, the
  greed influence 93